CURIOSITIES SERIES

Washington
CURIOSITIES

QUIRKY CHARACTERS, ROADSIDE ODDITIES & OTHER OFFBEAT STUFF

HARRIET BASKAS

SECOND EDITION

INSIDERS' GUIDE®

GUILFORD, CONNECTICUT
AN IMPRINT OF THE GLOBE PEQUOT PRESS

To buy books in quantity for corporate use
or incentives, call **(800) 962–0973**
or e-mail **premiums@GlobePequot.com.**

Text design: Nancy Freeborn
Layout: Debbie Nicolais
Maps: created by Rusty Nelson © Morris Book Publishing, LLC

Library of Congress Cataloging-in-Publication Data is available.
ISBN: 978-0-7627-4235-6

Manufactured in the United States of America
Second Edition/First Printing

The prices, rates, and hours listed in this guidebook were confirmed
at press time. We recommend, however, that you call establishments
to obtain current information before traveling.

For Ross, partner in travel and all else.

WASHINGTON

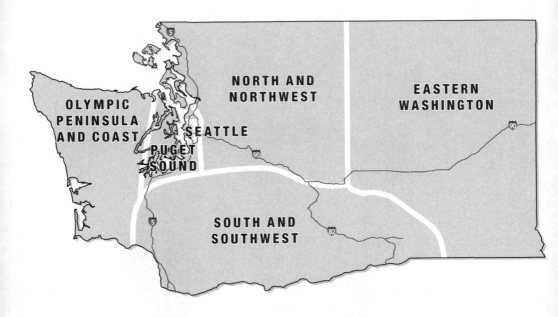

OLYMPIC PENINSULA AND COAST

NORTH AND NORTHWEST

EASTERN WASHINGTON

SEATTLE

PUGET SOUND

SOUTH AND SOUTHWEST

Contents

Acknowledgments

A giant thank-you to everyone who helped out with ideas, tips, photos, drawings, and generous encouragement for this project.

Introduction

I'm originally an East Coast kid, and unless I take up surfing or dogsledding and move to Hawaii or Alaska, I'm pretty sure I've hit my westernmost time zone. Although I can't imagine living anyplace else now, I have to admit that blending in among the Washingtonians took a while.

On my first visit to western Washington, I was taken aback by the discarded ripe bananas that people had irresponsibly left all along the lovely hiking trails in the woods. "Those aren't bananas," a smirking local told me. "Those are our famous banana slugs. They grow really big and they can get pretty darn far on that slime trail that they're oozing along on. Watch your step."

For my second visit, I approached by car from the east. It was 1980 and I'd driven cross-country in a red Volkswagen Rabbit with my husband-to-be. We'd made our way through miles of potholes in Ohio, stopped for that much-hyped free water at Wall Drug, and snaked our way through endless snowy mountain passes. At the Washington border, though, things got murky. It looked to me like eastern Washington was full of dirt. "My goodness," I blurted out, "you'd think they'd sweep up the fields out here every once in a while."

"Young lady," a gas station attendant several miles down the road gently informed me, "that's not dirt, that's piles of ash left over from the Mount St. Helens eruption. There's so much of it we just don't have anywhere to put it."

I've been gently set straight several times since then, and I've been consistently amused and bemused by the people, places, roadside attractions, and offbeat events I've encountered in Washington. It's not as if I haven't encountered the unusual elsewhere. I've been roaming the United States for the better part of twenty-five years, reporting on odd museums and people with curious collections for radio, newspapers, and books. I can tell you about the monastery that harbors a giant hairball, the location of an extensive collection of shrunken heads, and where to see intricate patriotic portraits made from thousands of common bugs. It's just that researching and writing this book finally gave me an extra excuse to delve deeply into the eccentric side of my adopted home state. And although I thought I knew the whereabouts of everything weird in Washington, I was pleasantly surprised to find out just how much I didn't know.

For example, researching this book helped me locate, once and for all, the town with a shrine to the Jolly Green Giant, the man who keeps a collection of more than 2,500 mechanical robots in a "hut" bigger than his house, and the roadside rest stop that is the new home of the much-loved drive-through tree stump. I also learned that other names in the running for Washington State were Tahoma, Columbia, and Washingtonia, and that the folks in the places we now know as Minnesota and Mississippi had also toyed with taking the name of the country's first president as their state name.

Carving into Washington State's curiosities has been great fun, and to tell you the truth, I wasn't looking forward to the manuscript delivery deadline. Not because I hate endings, but because every day brings news of yet another person or place or event that I want to tell you about.

The line had to be drawn somewhere, though, so as you flip through the pages of *Washington Curiosities,* you'll discover more than 200 of the unusual people, places, and things that make Washington such a kooky and endearing place.

Just watch your step around those banana slugs.

SEATTLE

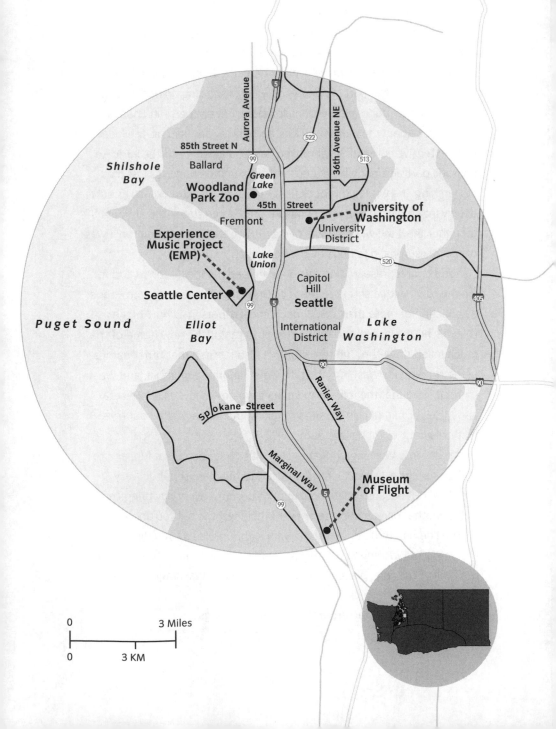

SEATTLE

Seattle, the most densely populated city in Washington State, has adopted the moniker Emerald City in honor of its lush surroundings. The lushness is courtesy of the climate, which is actually drier than you've been led to believe: Less rain falls in Seattle than in New York or Chicago. It just drizzles a lot here, so the inches of rainfall take a long time to accumulate.

Even before Seattleites got the reputation for being fueled by lattes, they were brimming with ideas. Back in 1889, after a fire gutted the downtown area, locals agreed to raise the rebuilt streets so that the toilets wouldn't back up when the tide came in. Later, Seattle became the first city to send police out on those streets on bicycles. Seattle is also the city where skywriting was invented and where the nation's first gasoline pump dispensed fuel to early motorists. It's also a city on the move: After the February 2001 earthquake, Seattle ended up five and a half millimeters closer to Vancouver, British Columbia.

Don't worry, though, Seattle is still easy to find. And so is the downtown shrine to oversize footwear, the neighborhood troll who lives under a bridge, the long-defunct but much loved gas station in the shape of a cowboy hat and a pair of giant boots, and all sorts of other curiosities.

Don't You Want Any of These?
Seattle

Know anyone who has covered a dashboard, coffee table, or desktop with mini aliens, rubber spiders, pink plastic flamingos, or teeny-weeny robots? Have a friend who has suddenly started sporting tiny record-player earrings or carrying a lunchbox adorned with kitschy sayings? These people have probably gotten ahold of the Archie McPhee catalog or spent an afternoon browsing the aisles at the company's enter-taining store in the Ballard neighborhood.

No telling who you'll meet while shopping at Archie McPhee.

This wonderland of weird and witty whatnots offers a bevy of bins filled with windup toys, party favors, plastic charms, and rubber creatures of all shapes and sizes. It's all mixed and matched with collectible character dolls, a great array of novelty candies, and barrels of leftover gears, gaskets, and geegaws so intriguing you'll decide to take home a bagful, despite having no idea exactly what it is you've bought.

This is the place to head to if you need fun stuff to put in those birthday party gift bags, goofy gifts to hand out at the office, or costumes and decorations for Halloween or just about any other holiday.

Bring some kids if you feel you might need an excuse to act silly as you shop, but most afternoons you'll find the place filled with adults giggling on their own in the aisles. And that includes the folks who work here.

Archie McPhee is located at 2428 Northwest Market Street in Ballard. Just look for the store with a giant lizard head over the front door. And be sure to visit the Archie McPhee annex next door, which is filled with all the oddly oversized objects that just don't fit in the main store. For hours call (206) 297-0240 or check the store's Web site, www.mcphee.com.

On the Lookout for a Yellow Submarine
Seattle

Built to welcome visitors to the 1962 Seattle World's Fair and perched on Pier 67 overlooking Elliott Bay and the Olympic Mountains, the Edgewater Hotel has attained waterfront landmark status. In addition to its great location, the inn also sports a popular restaurant and a giant red neon "E" on the rooftop that offers direction to ships navigating Puget Sound.

For music fans, however, the allure of the Edgewater is Room 272. When the Beatles stopped to play a much-heralded concert in Seattle during their first American tour, the Fab Four stayed at the Edgewater. Like many of the guests at that time, the cheeky chaps took the opportunity provided by the hotel's waterfront location to go fishing out the window. No one remembers if those crazy mop-tops caught anything, but pictures of John, Paul, George, and Ringo enjoying a rare moment of relaxation hit the newswires.

After the Beatles put the Edgewater on the map, musicians ranging from the Rolling Stones and Frank Zappa to José Feliciano and the Village People insisted on staying here as well. Today Room 272, now officially dubbed the Beatles Suite, is available for rent to musicians and fans alike, but although the hotel offered fishing licenses and fishing rods for sale at the gift shop until the mid-1980s, these days fishing out the window is no longer allowed.

The Edgewater Hotel is located at 2411 Alaskan Way, on Pier 67. For information call (206) 728-7000 or visit www.edgewaterhotel.com.

Maybe those crazy mop-tops didn't realize there was a restaurant at their hotel.

BEST PLACE TO HAVE A HEART ATTACK

Of course, no one wants to have a heart attack, but if you're going to have one, head for Seattle. That's because the city not only boasts one of the country's highest rates of Red Cross CPR training, there's also a local ordinance that offers legal immunity to someone who tries to use CPR to help out a heart attack victim.

Concern for the heart is a tradition here. Back in 1992, Seattle was one of the first cities in the nation to make defibrillators a mandatory piece of equipment in all its emergency rescue vehicles.

Bobo's Back

Seattle

One of Seattle's best-loved icons recently came out of the closet. Now that this burly 6½-foot-tall guy is fluffed, buffed, and repainted, he stands bright-eyed and ready for happy reunions with all his old friends.

The big guy we're talking about is Bobo, a gorilla who lived with a human family for several years before moving to Seattle's Woodland Park Zoo and stealing the heart of every kid and adult who wandered by.

In 1951, when he was just two weeks old, Bobo was captured in Africa and brought back to the United States by a gorilla hunter named William "Gorilla Bill" Said. When he was four months old, Bobo was sold to Bill Lowman, who brought the baby gorilla home to live with his family in Anacortes. Bobo became an official member of the Lowman family, eating at the dinner table and taking daily baths. He wore diapers and children's clothing, and was eventually partially toilet trained. Bobo also had hobbies: He liked listening to music (especially Kate Smith), and he seemed to enjoy playing the piano and teasing Rusty, the family dog.

Folks who loved visiting Bobo at the zoo can still visit him—but now he's stuffed.

The gorilla was also a neighborhood tourist attraction, prompting visitors to stop by and look in the windows of the Lowmans' home at all hours of the day and night. Bobo was even profiled in *Life* magazine, on television, and in newspapers.

It wasn't long, though, before Bobo got too big for his britches. Literally. Bobo was a western lowland gorilla, the kind of gorilla that grows to be more than 6 feet tall and can weigh up to 600 pounds. Not exactly the type of housemate who could be expected to walk delicately through a house without breaking a chair, a table, or the bed. And although they tried to accommodate Bobo as he grew stronger, more inquisitive, and increasingly destructive, the Lowmans finally acknowledged that their two-and-a-half-year-old, sixty-pound "baby" gorilla could be better cared for at the zoo.

The separation was difficult for both the family and the gorilla, but eventually Bobo settled in at his new home and was embraced by a new and bigger family: pretty much everyone in Seattle. In fact, Bobo was so well loved by the Seattle community that when the gorilla died in the winter of 1968 at age sixteen, zoo officials allegedly held the news until well after Christmas in an effort to avoid breaking hearts citywide.

Bobo never really went away, because zoo officials had him stuffed, standing up on his legs (not a natural gorilla stance), and placed on display at Seattle's Museum of History and Industry (MOHAI). Over the next twenty years, kids who had grown up visiting Bobo at the zoo continued to visit him, although some did it under the guise of being there to keep an eye on their own kids.

By the late 1990s Bobo was rather worn. His fur had gotten dull and a bit ratty, so museum officials put the gorilla in storage. That didn't stop folks from asking—and sometimes demanding—to see their old friend. Eventually Bobo was sent back to the taxidermist for a complete refurbishing.

Now, to the delight of kids and adults throughout the region, a fresh-looking Bobo is back on display at MOHAI in an exhibit titled *Gorilla in Our Midst*. He's in a glass exhibit case surrounded by photographs, news clippings, his baby bottle and rattle, and clothing he was dressed in as a young gorilla, including an impossibly small pair of overalls.

You can see Bobo at Seattle's Museum of History and Industry, at 2700 24th Avenue East, in McCurdy Park near the University of Washington. Phone (206) 324-1126 or log on to www.seattle.history.org. To see live gorillas, head over to the Woodland Park Zoo (206-684-4800, www.zoo.org) at 5500 Phinney Avenue North between North 50th and North 59th Streets, where there are two gorilla groups living in the tropical rain forest.

Bruce Lee's Grave
Seattle

In 1993 the Associated Press reported that three martial arts enthusiasts had walked 3,700 miles from Mongolia so they could pay homage to Bruce Lee at his grave site in Seattle on what would have been the kung fu legend's fifty-third birthday. The trio flew across the Bering Strait, courtesy of donations contributed by other Lee fans, but during the hiking part of their seven-month trek they wore out multiple pairs of boots.

Why all the fuss? Bruce Lee established a highly respected branch of martial arts called Jeet Kune Do and starred in several well-known kung fu movies, including *Enter the Dragon* and *Fists of Fury*. The martial arts master died in 1973 and was buried in Seattle, where he had spent a good deal of his childhood. Lee's son, Brandon, who died in a freak accident on the set of the martial arts movie *The Crow* in 1993, is buried alongside his dad in Seattle's prestigious Lakeview Memorial Cemetery. The picturesque cemetery is also the final resting spot for many of the city's founding fathers, including Denny Maynard and Mercer Yesler.

Each day the Lee plots receive about fifty visitors, many of whom leave notes and tokens of remembrance at the graves. Lakeview Memorial Cemetery is located at 1554 15th Avenue East in the Capitol Hill neighborhood, adjacent to Volunteer Park. To find the grave sites of Bruce and Brandon Lee, head straight up the hill from the main gate, toward the flagpole at the top of the hill. The graves are just a bit northeast of the flagpole. Phone (206) 322-1582.

High-Style Hen Homes
Seattle

Seattle is one of the few major cities where you're allowed to keep chickens in your yard. Don't start dreaming about setting up an urban chicken ranch just yet, though. Flocks are limited to just three hens, and both the city and your neighbors would prefer it if you'd steer away from keeping roosters, nature's early rising, all-natural alarm clocks.

Some inner-city chickens have high-style digs.

Despite the restrictions, chickens and chicken coops of all sizes and styles are popping up in yards throughout the city. Dogs and cats, of course, remain popular companions, but, increasingly, chicken owners can be heard crowing about how their poultry pets do double duty by providing fresh eggs and plenty of entertainment.

To celebrate the popularity of this egg-citing hobby and to educate others about the charms of urban chicken farming, Seattle Tilth, an organic gardening association, teaches poultry-raising classes and sells chicken-raising manuals and do-it-yourself coop plans. On occasion the organization has also offered urban chicken coop tours that take folks to some truly egg-centric in-city coops.

So how creative do folks get on behalf of their chickens? Well, past tours have featured architect-designed henhouses, elaborately decorated poultry penthouses, a chicken chalet, and detailing that ranges from an Old West storefront to stained-glass windows. Marmalade, Treacle, and the other chickens in Ray Nichol's flock, for example, live in a 6-foot-tall, multilevel structure that's been called the Camp David of chicken coops. It has a shake roof, and its windows are decorated with sandblasted images of—you guessed it—chickens.

To find out more about keeping chickens in a city, building roosts that even your neighbors will rave about, and dates for upcoming tours, call (206) 633-0451 or hunt-and-peck this Web address on your keyboard: www.seattletilth.org.

CHICKEN NUGGETS

Why did the chicken cross the road? Seattle Tilth's Angelina Shell might know. She's been scratching around for all sorts of chicken-related nuggets:

• Not all eggs are white: Araucana and Ameraucana pullets lay light blue and green eggs!

• To be perfectly correct: Pullets and hens are female chickens; roosters are male.

• Chickens, which are actually a type of pheasant, can lay an egg a day in the right conditions and do NOT need roosters to lay.

• Chickens are very curious. They like to know what's going on and can be trained to come when called.

• Female chickens only crow or cackle after they have laid an egg. It's the nonlaying roosters that you hear crowing at 5:00 a.m.!

Best Seat in the House

Seattle

At 997 feet the Bank of America Tower is Seattle's tallest building and the tallest, by number of floors, of any building west of the Mississippi. It was supposed to be even taller, but the Federal Aviation Administration made the architects shave 8 feet off their 1,005-foot design due to concerns about interference with the flight path into SeaTac Airport. By snipping just a few inches off each floor, they managed to retain the original seventy-six-story design.

The award-winning view from the women's room on the seventy-sixth floor of the Bank of America Tower.

On a clear day you can get great views of the surrounding mountain ranges and the city skyline from many of the building's 8,816 windows. Those in the know, however, say the building's best views are offered up to folks lucky enough to get a seat in one of the four stalls of the women's restroom at the members-only Columbia Tower Club on the seventy-sixth floor. Each stall has its own floor-to-ceiling window that offers stall occupants a great view of the Cascade Mountains or, on overcast days, the clouds. The experience is so unusual that this private privy consistently garners nominations for "America's Best Bathroom."

You'll need to fork over a membership (or make friends with a club member) in order to visit the Columbia Tower Club's women's restroom. On weekdays, however, nonmembers can pay the modest admission fee and wend their way up to Observation Deck, which wraps most of the way around the tower's seventy-third floor, just three stories below. The views from up there are pretty much the same as those from the women's room at the Columbia Tower Club, but here you don't have to worry about getting toilet paper stuck on your shoe.

The Bank of America Tower is located at 710 Fifth Avenue, at the corner of Columbia Street; phone (206) 386-5151. For information about the Columbia Tower Club, call (206) 622-2010 or log on to www .columbia-tower.com.

It's a Car! It's a Plane! No, It's a Car *and* a Plane!

Seattle

Moulton ("Molt") B. Taylor of Longview, Washington, was a guy who didn't like traffic jams. In the late 1940s this inventor, navy pilot, and missile designer developed what is still every commuter's dream come true: a flying automobile. Christened the Aerocar, the small two-passenger vehicle came with a rear propeller and a set of wings. These could easily be towed behind the car on the highway, and just as easily attached for flight should the driver encounter a traffic jam en route.

Taylor built several versions of his Aerocar; although each was airworthy, deals with the Ford Motor Company and others to massproduce the mixed-form transit unit never quite got off the ground. Still, there were some converts. Bob Cummings, an actor who starred in early TV sitcoms, owned an Aerocar, which made an appearance in one of the late-1950s episodes of *The Bob Cummings Show*. And Cummings

The Aerocar: a commuter's dream vehicle come true.

didn't keep the Aerocar to himself. He gave rides to his Hollywood dates, among them Marilyn Monroe.

Today the Aerocar III, Taylor's sixth and final car, is on display at the Museum of Flight, next to Boeing Field in Seattle. The museum also displays a few other great getaway vehicles, including the original Presidential Air Force One (a Boeing VC-137B), a recently retired British Airways Concorde, and the Apollo command module that astronauts used for splashdown practice. After its training stint, this module spent a decade abandoned and abused in a Houston Department of Public Works equipment lot before being rescued and restored.

The Museum of Flight is located at 9404 East Marginal Way South. For more information phone (206) 764-5720 or visit www.museumof flight.org.

Who Goes There?
Seattle

There's always been a strong connection between travelers and trolls. In childhood, many of us shivered at the story of the Three Billy Goats Gruff, who encountered and eventually outsmarted an evil and ugly troll living under a bridge. In other cultures mean-spirited trolls with all sorts of magical powers show up as well, with housing arrangements that range from caves and forests to oceans and, of course, bridges.

Building on the troll tradition and seeking some sort of artwork for the dimly lit Fremont side of the Aurora Bridge, the Fremont Arts Council commissioned a shaggy but friendly 17-foot-tall troll from a four-member team of Seattle-area artists in 1989. Working with rebar, wire, two tons of concrete, a hubcap, and a real Volkswagen Beetle, the team completed the troll on-site in seven weeks.

Rather than scaring folks who venture too close, the troll has become a much-loved part of the community. People leave flowers for the troll and scramble up to have their picture taken perched on top of his head. Once a year, on Halloween, the troll is the kickoff point for a grand neighborhood celebration called Trollaween, which includes a parade, costumed revelers, art installations, and a wide variety of planned and impromptu performance pieces.

You can visit the troll underneath the north end of the Aurora Avenue Bridge, at North 36th Street and Aurora Place North.

Proof that trolls really do live under bridges.

Group Wave

Seattle

Anyone who's attended a sports event in the past, say, twenty-five years, has no doubt been swept up in the audience-participation activity known as the "human wave" or the "audience wave." That's the goofy but visually intriguing group exercise in which fans stand up and sit down (or just raise and lower their arms) in a domino-like effect that rolls around the stadium.

Folks at Washington University in St. Louis and as far away as Brazil have tried to lay claim to being the creators of this craze, but according to the folks in the Athletic Department at the University of Washington in Seattle, the origins of the human wave can be traced to a football game played at the school's Husky Stadium on October 31, 1981. On that day a former cheerleader named Rob Weller (who went on to be a cohost on the *Entertainment Tonight* TV program) was in town for a visit. From the sidelines he is said to have instructed the crowd in one section to start waving and then had the audience roll the wave around the stadium.

The unusual sight may have unnerved the visiting team. According to a statement from University of Washington officials, "The Wave is believed to have started in the third quarter as the Huskies reeled off 28 points in route to a 42–31 win over the John Elway led Stanford team."

FIRST FILLING STATION

In the early days of motoring, gasoline was sold down at the general store. Horseless carriage owners bought wooden boxes containing two five-gallon cans of gas, toted them home, and then filled their tanks as needed.

In 1907 John McLean figured out a better way to get this job done. While working in Seattle for one of the major oil companies, McLean came up with the idea of dispensing gasoline directly into cars from a large storage tank, eliminating the need for individual shopkeepers to maintain a separate outbuilding to store small tanks of gas.

Today's gas stations can be elaborate affairs where travelers can eat, shop, bank, and shower while the tank is being filled, but the world's first gas station was much simpler. A feed line ran from a main storage tank to a 6-foot-tall, thirty-gallon container that had a glass gauge and a dispensing hose equipped with an on/off valve. No word on whether the attendant offered to check the oil and clean the windows.

One Giant Foot in Front of the Other

Seattle

As a young boy, Dan Eskenazi was understandably intrigued by the giant boots (size 37AA!) on display in his grandfather's downtown shoe repair shop window. The world's tallest man, 8-foot-11-inch Robert Wadlow, had given those boots to his grandfather on a promotional tour through town in the 1930s. Unfortunately, when Eskenazi's grandfather died in the 1960s, the giant shoes mysteriously disappeared from the store window. And they haven't been seen since.

Eskenazi now collects big shoes and is the curator of the Giant Shoe Museum in Seattle's Pike Place Market. Dedicated to the preservation of outsize and oversize footwear, the museum features Eskenazi's collection of more than twenty giant shoes arranged in a series of peep-show-inspired, coin-operated display windows.

Drop a quarter (or two) into the pay box, and velvet curtains open up to reveal the treasures, which include a 4-foot-long giant lace-up boot

Giant shoes were once a common sight on Seattle's waterfront.

originally displayed at the 1893 Chicago Exposition, the world's largest loafer, an enormous clown's shoe, the world's largest military boot, and a 3-foot-long wooden shoe adorned with a gold-leaf painting. Then there's "The Colossus," a 150-pound, 5-foot-long handmade black leather wingtip from the 1920s that Eskenazi believes may be the world's largest shoe.

"All these giant shoes," explains Eskenazi, "were display items once used in a shoe store window, as a promotional gimmick, or mounted on the roof of a delivery truck. They were well made, just like a regular-size shoe, only much, much bigger!"

The Giant Shoe Museum is located on the "down under" level of Seattle's Pike Place Market, just to the left of the Old Seattle Paperworks shop. For more information call (206) 623-2870.

Location, Location, Location
Seattle

Even if you've never been to Seattle, you've probably seen it. The city has had bit parts and starring roles in more than one hundred films and TV episodes and made its Hollywood debut in the 1933 film *Tugboat Annie,* whose stars included Maureen O'Sullivan, Wallace Beery, and Robert Young. Since then countless other celebrities, including Elvis, Tom Hanks, James Earl Jones, and Jennifer Lopez have come to town to film scenes, and visiting the locations made famous in those films is a popular pastime for locals and tourists alike.

Spots around town immortalized in films such as *Sleepless in Seattle* (with Tom Hanks and Meg Ryan), *It Happened at the World's Fair* (Elvis), and *The Fabulous Baker Boys* (with Michelle Pfeiffer and Jeff and Beau Bridges) are all listed on a handy free map put together by the folks at the Mayor's Office of Film and Video. In addition to listing the location of dozens of scenes that have taken place in popular locations around town (e.g., both Elvis and Sylvester Stallone filmed scenes on the monorail), the map includes a *Sleepless in Seattle* tour with directions to more than a half-dozen spots seen in the film.

The map also includes a tantalizing list of other Washington State towns and cities that have appeared in films and TV episodes, most notably the still popular locations around Snoqualmie and North Bend that were used in David Lynch's *Twin Peaks* television series and movie, and many others.

The map is available at many downtown Seattle hotels, at the downtown branch of the Seattle Public Library, at visitor information desks at the Washington State Convention Center, at other locations around town, and online at www4.seattle.gov/filmoffice/docs/map.pdf.

Honoring Hendrix
Seattle

James M. "Jimi" Hendrix was born in Seattle in 1942 and died in London in 1970, at age twenty-seven, after overdosing on barbiturates. In between he revolutionized rock and roll, made great use of feedback, and ruined some perfectly good guitars. He also left us "Purple Haze," "Hey Joe," "Are You Experienced," and a slew of other classic rock hits. Around Seattle, there are a few spots where Hendrix fans flock to worship this rock icon.

On Capitol Hill (at Broadway Avenue near East Pine Street), there's a life-size bronze sculpture of Hendrix clutching a guitar. His eyes are shut, his head is thrown back, and it looks like we've come upon him mid-riff on a very good day for making music.

More intensive worship goes on in the first-floor Jimi Hendrix Gallery at the Experience Music Project (EMP), which owns the world's largest

Rock icon Jimi Hendrix is honored with a statue—and a wing in a museum.

collection of Hendrix memorabilia. Artifacts on display include fragments of the Fender Stratocaster guitar the musician smashed and burned at the Monterey International Pop Festival in June 1967, his signed contract for playing the Woodstock festival in July 1969, and the handwritten notes for *Electric Ladyland*. The EMP's Hendrix collection also includes the audio mixing board from the artist's Electric Lady recording studio and bits of the performer's clothing, including a felt hat and a kimono he wore at the Newport Pop Festival in June 1969.

The EMP has about 80,000 other artifacts in its collection, ranging from the very first electric guitar to turntables and stage apparel belonging to the top hip-hop and rap artists. Look for Bo Diddley's guitar, flowered bell-bottom pants worn by Janis Joplin, and song lyrics handwritten by Nirvana's Kurt Cobain, among other unique items. Although "only" about 1,200 of these artifacts are displayed at any one time, the multistory EMP also offers a sound lab where you can play a variety of rock instruments (alone or with others), a giant music-playing sculpture made from more than 500 guitars and other instruments, and the Sky Church concert hall, featuring the world's largest indoor video screen.

While the artifacts inside the EMP are exhilarating to music fans, it's the shiny EMP building itself that sparks just about everyone's curiosity. Designed by noted architect Frank Gehry, who was supposedly inspired by the undulating shape of an electric guitar, this colorful and curvaceous building is impossible to miss on the edge of Seattle Center.

The Jimi Hendrix Gallery is located inside the Experience Music Project at Seattle Center, right next to the amusement park on Fifth Avenue. Phone (206) 367-5483 or (877) 367-5483 or check out www.emplive.com.

ROCK ICON RESTING PLACE

Since his death in 1970, a visit to Jimi Hendrix's grave in Renton's Greenwood Memorial Park has become a "must-do" for rock fans of all ages. For years, Hendrix was buried beneath an unassuming ground-level marker bearing the words "Forever in Our Hearts." Recently, though, the Hendrix family built a large granite and marble memorial about 100 feet away from the original grave site. They exhumed Jimi's remains and reburied them in the new, more elaborate resting spot. You're likely to find the area sprinkled with gifts left by fans, ranging from guitar picks and flowers to photographs and the occasional joint. Feel free to sign the guest book at the cemetery office and leaf through the comments written by folks from around the world who've made the pilgrimage to Greenwood.

Greenwood Memorial Park is located on the east side of Renton, at 350 Monroe Avenue Northeast, about a half-hour drive south of Seattle; phone (425) 255-1511. Hendrix's grave is located toward the back of the cemetery, past a pyramid and about 20 feet west of a sundial.

Don't Stop to Smell This Flower
Seattle

Botanists at the University of Washington have been repeatedly successful in coaxing one of the world's most reticent flowers to bloom. That's the good news. The bad news is, whenever this giant blooms, it really, really stinks. But then again, there's some good news: The bloom usually lasts for only four days, and that awful smell often dissipates after about twelve hours.

To make matters worse (or in some folks' minds, better), not only does this unusual flower stink, when it's in bloom the 5½-foot-tall plant sports what looks like an upside-down skirt and a giant phallic spike, or spadix, sticking up from the center.

The *Amorphophallus titanum,* better known as the corpse flower because, well, that's what folks think of when they smell it, actually uses its putrid aroma to attract flies, carrion beetles, and other insects. The olfactory-challenged insects crawl inside the plant and hang out for a day or two, wallowing in pollen. Then, when the giant spike starts to wither and the smell begins to fade, the insects hightail it out of there and set out to pollinate other plants.

In its natural habitat, in Indonesia's Sumatra, the plant has become scarce due to farming, logging, and the fact that some people consider it an aphrodisiac or a cure for impotence. In Seattle, the devil tongue, as it's been called, is simply a stinky attraction that makes some folks think of broccoli, overcooked cabbage soup, or, according to some police officers and medics who have stopped by, "definitely the smell of a human corpse."

If, despite that description, you still want to get up close to one of these giant foul-smelling flowers, you're in luck (if that's what you want to call it). University of Washington botanists now have almost a dozen corpse flower seedlings that, between them all, generate up to four

Big and stinky!

flowerings a year. When a blossom is nearing its peak, the public is welcome to come by and inhale. In past years public sniffings have taken place at the university's greenhouse, but because so many people wish to whiff, blooming corpse flowers are often put on view at the Conservatory in Seattle's Volunteer Park.

To find out when the corpse flower's next blooming is expected and if a public smelling is planned, call the greenhouse at (206) 543-0436 or check their Web site: dcpts.washington.edu/biology/greenhouse/. The university's Visitor Information Center is located at the southeast corner of University Way and Campus Parkway in Seattle. Seattle's Volunteer Park Conservatory is open year-round and is located at 1400 East Galer Street. For directions and more information call (260) 684-4743 or visit their Web site at www.seattle.gov/PARKS/parkspaces/Volunteer Park/conservatory.htm.

What's He Doing Here?
Seattle

Controversial and hard to avoid, a seven-ton cast bronze sculpture of Vladimir Lenin presides over a busy corner of Fremont, Seattle's most eccentric and whimsical neighborhood.

Who is he, and how did he get here?

Vladimir Lenin, Marxist theoretician and father of modern communism, was the founder of the Bolshevik movement, a leader of the 1917 Russian Revolution, and the first premier of the USSR. History books portray him by turns as a radical intellectual concerned with workers' rights and reform and a ruthless dictator whose policies led to the oppression and starvation of millions.

The statue, created by Slavic artist Emil Venkov, was originally installed in Poprad, Slovakia, in 1988. After the 1989 revolution, however, the sculpture ended up facedown in the street. That's how Lewis Carpenter, a Seattle-area citizen teaching in Poprad, came upon it. After deciding to salvage the sculpture, he somehow got it shipped to his home in Issaquah, Washington, where it sat for a while in a field. Shortly after Carpenter died in 1994, his family loaned the Lenin statue to the Fremont neighborhood, where it will sit until a buyer or a more suitable home is found. As you can imagine, this statue elicits a wide range of responses from passersby. Some applaud the work as a piece of public art that, good or bad, evokes strong feelings. Others view it as proof that art outlives politics. You can decide for yourself. Emil Venkov's statue of Vladimir Lenin surrounded by guns and flames leans forward from its perch at North 36th Street and Evanston Avenue.

Where do you put a seven-ton statue? Anywhere it fits.

Lutefisk Lovers
Seattle

Lutefisk, a dish prepared by treating dried cod with lye so that it yields something white and gelatinous, is a traditional Yuletide delicacy in places like Norway, Denmark, Sweden, and Seattle's Scandinavian-rooted Ballard neighborhood. Enjoying this food is surely an acquired taste: Devotees rave and reminisce about great lutefisk they've encountered, while detractors give it a very wide berth.

So we can only assume that the dozen or so contestants who choose to participate in the lutefisk-eating contest at the Ballard Seafood Fest each July are true-blue Scandinavians. If not, they must be completely out of their minds.

On the face of it, it seems as if it would be as easy as shooting fish in a barrel to win the cash prize. Simply eat more lutefisk than anyone else in the time allotted. The catch? The winner has to keep all that lutefisk down. Not an easy thing to do, considering the consistency and ingredients of the very white fish lying out there in the hot sun.

You don't need to watch these guys (for some reason it's usually all guys) gorging on lutefisk to enjoy the Ballard Seafood Fest. The annual street party also features several outdoor music stages, a bevy of food and craft booths, a kids' corner, a watermelon-eating contest, and a couture coverall contest. There's also a salmon barbecue. Now that's a fish we can sink our teeth into.

The Ballard Seafood Fest is held every July on the streets around 22nd Avenue Northwest and Northwest Market Street. For more information phone (206) 784-9705 or visit www.seafoodfest.org.

DO YOU SEE WHAT I SEE?

Let's say you're driving home late one night and you see a shiny object zipping around through the sky and it does not look at all like a plane. What do you do?

A. Race home and tell your spouse.
B. Call the police and the local newspaper.
C. Shake your head and keep telling yourself, "I didn't see a thing."

Peter Davenport, who operates the National UFO Reporting Center out of his Seattle apartment, would probably say, "D. None of the above." He'd rather you do what more than a thousand fellow "spotters" do every year: call the UFO Reporting Center's hotline at (206) 722-3000 to report the sighting, or log on to www.ufocenter.com to write up the experience, perhaps with an accompanying drawing or photograph.

Here's an excerpt from the National UFO Reporting Center Form:

Characteristics of Object (Check all that apply):

There were lights on the object
The object left a trail

There was an aura or haze around the object
The object emitted other objects
The object emitted beams
The object changed color
The object landed
The object made a sound
There were aircraft in the vicinity, or aircraft chasing the object
There were electrical or magnetic effects, such as a car engine stopping

In operation since 1974, the National UFO Reporting Center hasn't yet obtained undisputable proof of outer-space visitations, but Davenport, who calls himself an "alien hunter," says the sheer number of sighting reports from around the world more than convinces him that we are definitely not alone in the universe.

Why is he so sure? Well, since seeing his first UFO near the St. Louis municipal airport in 1954, Davenport has been witness to several "anomalous events," including several sightings in the early 1990s in California and in Washington State.

Perfectly Preserved Bathhouse
Seattle

Smaller and less intense than San Francisco's Chinatown, Seattle's International District has its own long and colorful history as the home of people from Japan, China, Korea, Vietnam, and other Asian countries. You can easily experience a multicultural afternoon simply by wandering the streets, visiting the diverse shops and restaurants, shopping at the Asian groceries, and exploring the various cultural institutions.

Be sure you don't miss the Panama Hotel. Dating from the early 1900s, the brick building was home to many immigrant workers in the days when this area was Seattle's Nihonmachi, or Japantown. Recently reopened and renovated, the building's basement houses one of the best-preserved Japanese public bath facilities, or sento, on the West Coast.

These baths were not merely a place to get clean; they provided a venue for members of the community to meet, socialize, relax, and participate in a cultural tradition that reaches back to the 1500s.

Known as Hashidate-Yu, the bathhouse at the Panama Hotel served the greater Seattle Japanese community from 1910 until the mid-1960s, closing temporarily when many Japanese citizens were sent to government internment camps during World War II.

Today visitors to the Panama Hotel can arrange to tour the well-preserved bathhouse and see facilities that have remained intact and untouched since it officially closed its doors to the public. The tubs and tile floors are still here, as are the changing rooms, lockers, signs telling customers where to put their shoes and towels, and vintage ads for area businesses.

The first floor of the Panama Hotel also contains a teahouse, its walls decorated with photographs depicting the community's rich history. Head to the back, where a window cut into the floor offers a view of the basement, which is filled with suitcases, clothing, pots, pans, and other unclaimed personal items stored and then left behind by Japanese citizens when they were forced into the internment camps. Many of these people never returned for their possessions, and the current hotel owner decided to save and display these poignant items rather than throw them away.

The Panama Hotel is located at 605 South Main Street, in Seattle's International District. For more information about hours and to arrange a tour of the bathhouse, call (206) 223-9242 or check out www.panama hotel.net.

Don't Look Now
Seattle

If you've already seen the major city sights and you're feeling a bit curious about some of the less touristy (and at times downright grisly) aspects of the Emerald City, sign up for one of the guided van tours offered by Private Eye on Seattle.

Your guide for each two-hour tour is Jake, a Seattle native with an interest in forensics, a background in medicine and science, and a strong attraction to the macabre. Hop into her blood-red van and she'll take you to visit notorious crime scenes and murder sites, haunted spots, and the homes and final resting places of a variety of celebrities.

Drawing on case files that go back almost fifty years, the Queen Anne tour stops at former bordellos and speakeasies, the site of the Wah Mee massacre, and the spot where a $2 million heist occurred. The Capitol Hill tour includes visits to the former home of murderer Ted Bundy, the house where musician Kurt Cobain lived and eventually committed suicide, and the Lake View cemetery, which is the final resting place of Bruce Lee and his son Brandon Lee. If that's not creepy enough for you, Private Eye on Seattle also offers a van tour of many of Seattle's haunted places, with stops at a mortuary, a theater, a hotel, a rooming house, and an old burial ground.

If you've got kids with you or if you tend to be a bit squeamish, you might want to skip these tours. But if you're interested in finding out a bit about some of the city's more ghoulish and gruesome events, hop on board.

For information about rates and reservations, call (206) 365-3739 or check out www.privateeyetours.com.

Outdoor Adventures Indoors
Seattle

Sure, REI's 80,000-square-foot flagship store near downtown Seattle draws a lot of healthy-looking, active, outdoorsy folks looking for sleeping bags, mountain bikes, and all sorts of hiking and mountaineering gear to take with them on their next trip out into the Northwest wilderness. The place also draws a lot of indoorsy types just looking for an afternoon of adventure and entertainment.

You can test out hiking boots or mountain bikes on the store's easy-to-traverse outdoor loop trail. If that saps your energy, take a break at the espresso bar and then wander into the auditorium, where you might catch a free or low-cost clinic or presentation about all manner of outdoor activities you might someday attempt. Or you can cut to the chase and head straight for the pinnacle inside the front door.

Visible from the interstate, REI's glass-walled, 65-foot pinnacle—the world's tallest freestanding indoor climbing structure—offers climbing opportunities for all levels and abilities. You can watch others as they struggle to make their way to the top, sign up to try it yourself, or block out a few hours and come back with your club or organization so you can all hang around up there together. The climbing wall is awfully popular, so you'll probably need to call ahead for a reservation.

REI's Seattle store is located at 222 Yale Avenue, just off of Interstate 5. For hours, fees, and directions, phone (206) 223-1944 or visit www.rei.com/stores/seattle.

Ride the Elevator, Sit in a Chair, Get Married
Seattle

When it opened on July 4, 1914, Seattle's forty-two-story Smith Tower was the tallest building west of the Mississippi. Although it gave up that claim to fame fifty years later, the tower is still full of romance, class, and a bit of mystery.

The ornate Smith Tower was built at a cost of $1 million by Burns Lyman Smith, who got the money from his dad, Lyman Cornelius Smith, of Smith-Corona typewriter and Smith rifle fame. Constructed of Washington fir, granite, white terra-cotta, Alaskan marble, and Mexican onyx, the building contains 75 miles of wiring and enough fabricated steel to fill 164 railroad cars.

When it opened, the building had 540 "wired" offices, which in those days meant that each unit came complete with two telephone outlets, two telegraph outlets, 660 watts of electricity, and a vacuum cleaner. The office spaces have been reconfigured somewhat over the years, but the crown jewel of the Smith Tower remains. That would be the sumptuous Chinese Room on the thirty-fifth floor. Furnished by the last Empress of China as a gift to Mr. Smith, this room features a hand-carved wood and porcelain-inlay ceiling, ornately carved blackwood furniture, and fine works of art. An outdoor observation deck wraps around all four sides. Most intriguing is the Wishing Chair: Legend has it that any young woman who sits in the chair will be married within one year.

Even if you're already married or are intent on staying single, it's worth paying the admission fee to take the elevator ride up to the thirty-fifth floor. That's because six of the seven original brass-and-copper-caged Otis elevators are still here (powered by their original DC motors), the last manually operated elevators on the West Coast.

The Smith Tower is located at 506 Second Avenue, at the northeast corner of Yesler Way, in downtown Seattle. Self-guided tours of the Chinese Room, the observation deck, and the ornate entrance lobby are offered daily from April through October and on weekends the rest of the year. For more information call (206) 622-4004 or visit www .smithtower.com.

Kicking Off the Summer with Style
Seattle

Seattle's Fremont neighborhood, which bills itself as the "Center of the Universe," prides itself on its history of being funky and fun and pretty much ready for anything. At no other time is this more apparent than during the annual Fremont Solstice Parade, the grand Mardi Gras-style extravaganza that's been kicking off the annual Fremont Fair since 1989.

The fair is loads of fun, jam-packed as it is with concerts, food, arts and crafts booths, and all manner of street-fair-worthy activities. It's the parade, however, that offers the most curious sights, sounds, and outrageous experiences, and is the one summer kickoff event most people try not to miss.

Hosted by the enthusiastic Fremont Arts Council, which offers work-shops, advice, encouragement, and even materials to participants, the parade is populated by giant puppets, extravagantly decorated floats, colorful masks, imaginatively costumed characters, plenty of music, and usually a contingent of never sanctioned but always wildly popular and much applauded naked folks who show up on their bikes

The Fremont Solstice Parade kicks off the fair each year on the Satur-day of Summer Solstice Weekend along North 34th Street and Fremont Avenue. For more information phone (206) 547-7440 or visit www .fremontartscouncil.org/events/parade.html.

Big Head at rest.

Alien Landing Spot?
Seattle

Seattle's number one tourist destination is also one of the city's most unusual structures.

Originally built for the 1962 Seattle World's Fair, which had a futuristic twenty-first-century theme, the 605-foot-tall Space Needle is a long-limbed tower that has glass-fronted elevators crawling up and down its legs. At the top there's a flying-saucer-shaped dome with a 360-degree viewing deck and a rotating restaurant that is so perfectly balanced it requires nothing more than a 1½-horsepower electric motor to keep it turning. Although rotating restaurants are no longer all that unusual, the Space Needle was only the second revolving restaurant in the world. (The first one, now closed, was in the Ala Moana shopping mall in Hawaii.)

When it opened on the first day of the fair, the Space Needle was the tallest structure west of the Mississippi River. While taller buildings now pierce the skyline, the Space Needle remains the city's trademark image, with a slew of curious factoids all its own. Some highlights:

- The foundation for the Space Needle is 30 feet deep and 120 feet across.
- In less than twelve hours, 467 concrete trucks filled the space, in what was then the largest continuous concrete pour ever attempted in the West.
- The original plans called for a stork's nest on top of the Space Needle. That plan was scrapped when someone pointed out that storks couldn't survive in Seattle's climate.
- The Space Needle's elevators travel at a rate of 10 miles per hour or 800 feet per minute. As the fast-talking elevator operators like to say, that's as fast as a raindrop falls to Earth.

Land your spaceship or just ride the elevator to the top for a meal and the view.

- Some cities like the Space Needle so much, they want it. In fact, the nearby city of Fife once offered Seattle $1 million to move the structure to downtown Fife.

As you'd imagine, the Space Needle's gift shop is filled with all manner of Space Needle souvenirs, everything from Space Needle–shaped candles, cups, and costume jewelry to Space Needle–shaped pasta named, appropriately enough, Space Noodles. If those souvenirs don't strike your fancy, you can always go home and repaint your house with some of the colors spawned by the Space Needle decor, including Astronaut White, Orbital Olive, Re-entry Red, and Galaxy Gold.

The Space Needle is on the grounds of Seattle Center, at 400 Broad Street. For more information call (206) 905-2100 or visit www.space needle.com.

Straight to the Moon
Seattle

To the dismay of many local fans, the Rocket, a roadside attraction that once adorned a surplus store in downtown Seattle, was destined for the junkyard. A feisty group of local arts activists came to the rescue, but the Rocket ended up languishing in a back lot in the Fremont neighborhood for more than a year.

Finally, a team of "scientists," "metal specialists," and others was called together, and the Rocket was restored, complete with updated electronic features, structural details, and a new set of fins.

All prettied up, the Rocket touched down at its present site on a Fremont street corner in June 1994. It now bears the official crest and motto of the Fremont neighborhood, *De Libertas,* which means "freedom to be peculiar." And peculiar it is: Besides being an intriguing 53 feet tall, in the coin-operated "launch mode" the Rocket emits steam vapor from its base. Stick around long enough and you may even hear it emitting music and chat: Neighborhood folks envision turning the Rocket into a local FM radio station.

To see the Rocket, head for the corner of North 36th Street and Evanston Avenue in Fremont.

You Can Dress Them Up, But You Can't Move 'em
Seattle

Besides the Space Needle, Richard Beyer's 1979 *Waiting for the Interurban* sculpture is one of the most loved and most often photographed spots in town. Commemorating the Interurban Rail line that at one time connected downtown Seattle with the surrounding neighborhoods, the cast aluminum sculpture near the Fremont Bridge features a group of people and one dog . . . just waiting.

These folks and that dog have been waiting here since 1979.

Over the years *Waiting for the Interurban* has also become the city's most entertaining and interactive piece of public art. On any given day it's a good bet you'll find the sculpture decorated with a political banner or some colorful party decorations, with the "waiters" elaborately dressed up in hats, coats, scarves, dresses, and costumes in preparation for the weather or in celebration of a birthday, a wedding, a holiday, a marriage proposal, or some other special occasion.

The figures' faces are fairly nondescript, but neighborhood lore has it that the dog in the sculpture bears the likeness of Arman Napoleon, a local activist who once served as the unofficial mayor of the Fremont neighborhood.

You'll find Richard Beyer's *Waiting for the Interurban* sculpture in Seattle's Fremont neighborhood, just over the Fremont Bridge, on North 34th Street and Fremont Avenue North.

Enchanted Rockery
Seattle

In 1954 Milton Walker took his family on a car trip to Wenatchee to visit Ohme Gardens, a nine-acre park filled with trees, plants, rocks, and man-made lakes arranged in landscapes depicting everything from a rain forest to an alpine meadow. The little lakes, made of cement and painted blue, grabbed Milton Walker's imagination, so he tried to make one in his backyard when he got home.

That cement lake never did work out, but it gave Walker an idea that would eventually become an obsession. Using rocks he collected around the neighborhood and on trips to the beach, he built a little airport, a couple of small mountains, a landing strip, a miniature control tower, and, eventually, some lakes.

Milton Walker spent almost thirty years creating this fairy-tale rock garden in his backyard.

Not long after, when Walker came upon an Oregon rock shop going out of business, he purchased ten tons of stock for only $150. His family spent eleven weekends hauling home petrified wood, Brazilian agate, geodes, and other semiprecious stones. Then, armed with only a rock saw and his vivid imagination, Milton Walker began transforming what had been a terraced backyard on a hillside in a quiet residential Seattle neighborhood into a rock-encrusted wonderland.

Milton covered his patio with sliced agate. He faced the cement garden walls with stones. He built meandering cement pathways, and turned the vegetable patch into a growing mountain range.

How did he have time for all this? Walker volunteered for the swing shift at the Boeing factory so he'd have his daylight hours free for yard work. Vacations were spent gathering cobblestones, seashells, beach rock, and bits of colored glass.

When it came time for retirement, Walker was happy to spend night and day in the yard. That's when he built agate-studded benches, cement walls inlaid with glass butterflies, and a 20-foot-tall arched cement tower covered with a mosaic of glass and stone.

Milton Walker died in 1984, after spending more than thirty years creating the artwork in his backyard. Sadly, at the end of his life, the onset of Alzheimer's disease made him forget that he was the one who had built the garden; he thought maybe his sons had done it. His wife, Florence, said that he once told her the boys had done a very nice job.

For several years after his death, Milton Walker's family worked with a local nonprofit group to maintain the garden and host public tours. These days, the Walker family operates the garden alone. The garden is open to the public for free tours on Mother's Day and, during the summer, on Sundays from noon to 5:00 p.m., except on the first Sunday of the month. To schedule a visit at other times, call (206) 935-3036 or send an e-mail request to radams@smwireless.net.

Fill 'er Up and Snap That Brim

Seattle

These days, pretty much every gas station looks alike. Back in the mid-1950s, however, Seattle had a pump palace like no other. Designed by Lewis H. Nasmyth and engineered by Bruce Olsen, the Hat 'n' Boots Premium Tex Texaco gas station was a cowboy-themed extravaganza with an office in the shape of a giant red cowboy hat. The hat measured 44 feet across; a pair of 24-foot-tall, elaborately painted cowboy boots served as the station's restrooms.

Made of steel beams, chicken wire, and concrete, this roadside attraction was supposed to mark the entryway of Frontier Village, a shopping center with more than 200 shops that entrepreneur Buford Seals hoped to build. Seals went bust and the shopping center never materialized, but the Hat 'n' Boots kept pumping from its spot along State Route 99. In its prime, the Hat 'n' Boots was among the highest-grossing gas stations in the state, and legend even has it that Elvis Presley filled up his Cadillac here while in town to film *It Happened at the World's Fair* in 1963.

Unfortunately, the Hat 'n' Boots gas station closed down in 1988, and the eye-catching site lost its luster. Demolition was in the cards until residents of the surrounding Georgetown neighborhood rallied to rescue the down-at-the-heels structure. Local celebrities got involved, and in 1997 a demonstration featured protesters wearing—you guessed it—hats and boots.

Once a gas station, the Hat 'n' Boots now presides over a park.

The campaign worked. The Hat 'n' Boots was declared a Seattle land-mark in 2002, and funds were raised to allow the neighborhood to move the structures to a nearby vacant lot, which was then trans-formed into Oxbow Park. Restoration of the hat and the boots is now under way.

To see the Hat 'n' Boots in its new home, head to the 6400 block of Corson Avenue, next to B&G Machine, just off State Route 99 on the south end of Seattle. For more information visit www.hatnboots.org.

One Ringy-Dingy?

Seattle

Telephone switching equipment once filled entire buildings, but com-puters and satellites have made much of that old stuff, well, just old stuff. Lucky for us, some retired telephone workers, members of the wonderfully named Telephone Pioneers of America, just couldn't bear to have all that old equipment go to the junkyard.

Instead, they've created the Museum of Communications, dedicated to the evolution of the phone call, from Alexander Graham Bell's first communications device to the modern phones we can tuck into our pockets.

Tours begin on the third floor, and the guides are people who actu-ally installed and maintained this stuff, so you can ask questions about anything you see, from the switchboards to the historical photographs, the wide range of telephones, and even the working picture phone.

The second floor is where the real fun starts, though. Here you can crank the old phones, follow a phone call as it makes its way through a giant switching station, play at being a telephone operator, and exam-ine the variety of ingenious "slugs" and other objects folks have used in pay phones instead of real coinage.

Be sure to visit the Hewitt Room, which houses a collection of vintage telephones, each with a different ringer that will be rung enthusiastically. The collection belonged to Ted Hewitt, a general plant manager for Pacific Northwest Bell, who for years kept the imaginary central phone office for Timbuktu in his basement.

Another display here is dedicated to WECO (the Western Electric Company), the manufacturing arm of the Bell System that existed prior to 1984. In addition to telephones, WECO made hearing aids, fans, washing machines, sewing machines, radios, and vacuum cleaners. Who knew?

The Museum of Communications, located at 7000 East Marginal Way South, is open on Tuesdays and by special appointment. For more information call (206) 767-3012 or visit www.museumof communications.org.

No chance of missing a call with this giant Trimline phone.

Are You My Mummy?

Seattle

Robert Ripley, of *Ripley's Believe It or Not* fame, called Ye Olde Curiosity Shop and Museum "the greatest shop I ever got into." That's high praise for a place that's half souvenir shop and half wacky, offbeat museum.

Since 1899 Seattle visitors have flocked to some version of this store. They continue to come here not only to purchase Northwest crafts and souvenirs from around the world, but also to get a good look at the matchstick tugboat, the huge Puget Sound octopus, the record-size geoduck clam, the 9-foot blowgun, and the thousands of other odd items that cram the shelves, cover the walls, and hang from the ceiling.

The hands-down favorites among the overwhelming array of curiosities, though, are at the back of the shop. So be sure to make your way past the Space Needle salt-and-pepper sets, past the flatten-your-own-penny machine, past the wooden postcards, and beyond the plastic back scratchers. Up against the rear wall you'll find nightmare-inducing shrunken heads, stuffed and mounted twin calves, a pickled pig, and a petrified dog. And then there's Sylvia, the alarmed-looking mummy, and her sidekick, Sylvester, a long-dead prospector who, according to museum notes, was discovered perfectly preserved and dehydrated in the Arizona desert by two cowboys riding along and minding their own business back in 1895.

Ye Olde Curiosity Shop and Museum is located on Seattle's water-front at 1001 Alaskan Way, Pier 54. For hours and more information call (206) 682-5844 or visit www.yeoldecuriosityshop.com.

Strange and wondrous things hang around Ye Olde Curiosity Shop and Museum.

Extra Energy
Seattle

We're usually encouraged to stay away from utility company facilities, but Seattle's City Light welcomes one and all to visit the charming folk art display at one of its neighborhood substations.

Located around the corner from a busy intersection and just beyond a bank of hulking generators, there's a collection of colorful and wacky-looking windmills made out of everything from coffeepots and crankshafts to oil funnels and teacups. Protected by a chain-link fence, these creations all spin gleefully at the slightest puff of wind.

The amusing artwork was created by the late Emil Gehrke. He enjoyed driving around with his wife, Veva, in search of discarded junk that could be turned into perfectly balanced and highly entertaining whirligigs. More than one hundred of his creations are now planted in a windmill park just off a highway in Grand Coulee, but the twenty-seven pieces in the substation at Fremont Avenue North and North 105th Street offer plenty of amusement.

Emil Gehrke could turn just about anything into a wind thing.

OFFICIAL WASHINGTON

The Evergreen State has an official state song, "Washington, My Home," and an official state folk song, "Roll On, Columbia, Roll On," which was written by noted folksinger Woody Guthrie. The state also has an official fish, the steelhead trout; an official insect, the green darner dragonfly; and an official fruit, the apple. The state's official dance is the square dance, and the official state gem is, strangely enough, petrified wood. But although it is tree rich and incredibly green, Washington State didn't name the Western hemlock its official state tree until 1947.

Other official state symbols took a while to establish as well. For example, in 1928 legislators let schoolchildren vote for the state bird. The meadowlark won hands down. Unfortunately, the meadowlark was by then also the official bird of seven other states. So in 1931 another vote was taken, this time by the Washington Federation of Women's Clubs. The winner of this vote was the goldfinch, a delicate bird with a yellow body and black wings. It won out over nominees that included the woodpecker and the song sparrow. But now there were officially two state birds. So the legislature went back to the schoolchildren for a final decision, and in 1951 the goldfinch was chosen as the official, and permanent, state bird.

Here are some other official Washington State symbols:

State grass: bluebunch wheatgrass
State fossil: Columbian mammoth
State marine animal: orca
State flower: coast rhododendron (This flower was chosen by a vote of Washington State women in 1892, when an official flower was needed as an entry for the 1893 World's Fair in Chicago. However, it took until 1959 for the Washington State legislature to make it official.)
State vegetable: In 2007, thanks to a campaign mounted by several junior high school classes, the Walla Walla Sweet Onion was designated the state's official vegetable.

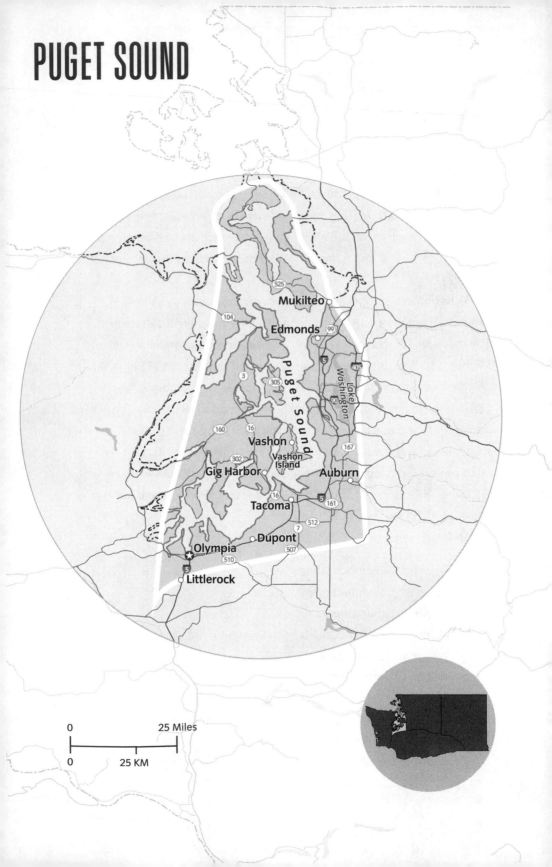

PUGET SOUND

Mukilteo

Edmonds

Puget Sound

Lake Washington

Vashon

Vashon Island

Gig Harbor

Auburn

Tacoma

Dupont

Olympia

Littlerock

525
104
99
5
405
3
305
50
160
16
167
302
16
5
161
7
512
507
510

0   25 Miles

0   25 KM

PUGET SOUND

Although the Puget Sound region officially stretches from north of Seattle all the way south to Olympia, this chapter focuses on the somewhat narrower swatch of territory that hugs the urban core.

That gives us room to meet folks such as Ann Mitchell Lovell, the curator of the Washington Banana Museum, and Bobj Berger, whose unusual collection of more than 200 rolls of toilet paper from around the world includes a roll of John Wayne-branded toilet paper bearing the slogan "It's rough, it's tough, and it don't take crap off nobody."

We also dip, very carefully, into the history of a Dupont, a company town built on dynamite. We'll scratch around for the story of Dot and Dash and the other well-trained racing roosters from Roosterville that helped put Gig Harbor on the map. And we learn the sad story of Galloping Gertie, the ill-fated, four-month-old Tacoma Narrows Bridge whose dramatic demise in a November 1940 windstorm was caught on film. As proof that Washingtonians are experts at making lemonade out of lemons, this spectacular sunken engineering failure was placed on the National Register of Historic places and now serves as one of the world's largest man-made reefs.

Old Flameful
Auburn

Yellowstone may have Old Faithful, but in Auburn the big draw is what some folks might call "Old Flameful." Well, to be honest, it's old, but these days it's not that flameful. In its better days, however, the natural wonder was so unusual that it was featured in *Ripley's Believe It or Not*.

The Flaming Geyser, as it's more formally known, gets its name from the methane gas flame that comes out of a pipe in the ground and burns 6 to 10 inches high. Truthfully, it's not that impressive, but old-timers tell tales of the days when the flame would roar several feet in the air, spurting out fire and water.

So where does the flame come from? In the early 1900s, when much of the land that is now the park was being mined for coal, one of the test pits produced a stream of methane gas and salty water. Someone lit a match, a flame blew 25 feet into the air, and the Flaming Geyser "attraction" was born. When mining tapered off, the riverfront and forest area around the Flaming Geyser became a private resort. After the resort went bankrupt in the 1960s, the state took over the property and created a public park.

Today rangers with matches are on hand to keep the Flaming Geyser lit and to explain the "mystery" of the geyser to visitors. The rangers can also direct the curious to the path that leads to the park's other, even smaller natural wonder, known as the Bubbling Geyser. Like the Flaming Geyser, the gurgling pool of water gets its geyser status from methane gas.

If trekking out to a park just to see a 6-inch flaming geyser doesn't spark your family's interest, try enticing them with the park's other features. The 480-acre Flaming Geyser State Park, part of the Green River Gorge Recreational Area, includes 10 miles of hiking trails and 5 miles of riverbank just perfect for white-water rafting, swimming, and fishing.

To get to the park, take State Route 18 to the Auburn–Black Diamond Road exit. Go east for ⅛ mile, turn right onto Green Valley Road, and continue 9 miles to the park entrance. For more information call (253) 931-3930 or check the Washington State Parks and Recreation Commission Web site at www.parks.wa.gov.

Banana Museum
Auburn

Ann Mitchell Lovell has had a long and happy fascination with bananas. When she was a kid, her parents called her Anna Banana. As an adult, on a trip to Hawaii in 1980 she picked up a few banana-related souvenirs. She later bought a few more banana-inspired items, then her friends began monkeying around, sending Lovell boatloads of banana things. Before she could say, "I'm going bananas," banana-themed toys, stuffed animals, signs, pottery, and other "bananabilia" were bunching up all over the house.

Rather than peel out, Lovell decided to stay put and turn her home into a shrine to the potassium-rich, yellow-jacketed fruit. With more than 4,000 banana things now in her collection, she herself has become something of a banana expert. Did you know, for example, that bananas were introduced to the American public at the 1876 Philadelphia Centennial Exposition, the very same event that introduced the world to Alexander Graham Bell's telephone? Anna Banana knows.

The museum includes banana paintings, drawings, and photographs; a history of the banana written for schoolchildren; books on bananas; banana-shaped lamps; earrings, necklaces, and other banana-inspired jewelry; and all manner of knickknacks in the shape of bananas, including teapots, cookie jars, salt-and-pepper shakers, and

Ann Mitchell Lovell loves all things banana.

more. And of course, Lovell's refrigerator is covered entirely with banana-themed magnets.

Advertisements for and media images of bananas abound, everything from Chiquita banana magazine spreads to Carmen Miranda dolls with headdresses full of bananas, and photos of Josephine Baker wearing a skirt made entirely of bananas. And while banana songs play on the stereo, Lovell can review her collection of movies, such as Woody Allen's *Bananas*, and sheet music for songs like "Yes, We Have No Bananas."

While Lovell may have the only banana museum in the Northwest, she's not alone in her passion for the fruit that arrives in the shape of a smile. Lovell is a card-carrying member of the International Banana Club, a self-proclaimed fun bunch that gets together every so often to swap banana artifacts and share banana-rich meals.

You can take a virtual tour of Ann Lovell's Washington Banana Museum at www.bananamuseum.com.

No Smoking Allowed
Dupont

In 1909 the E. I. du Pont de Nemours Company offered several nice perks to workers willing to move to "The Village," a company-owned town created in the forest near the company's plant south of Tacoma.

What later became the DuPont Company had built a neighborhood full of brand-new wooden frame houses that were wired for electricity and furnished with gas stoves, furnaces, and indoor plumbing. The town had a butcher shop, a church, a school, a hotel, several stores, and company-maintained parks and gardens. The town's doctor even dispensed free medicine.

The catch? The DuPont Powder Works made explosives, so everyone had to be very, very careful. How careful? Shoe heels had to be attached with wooden pegs rather than nails, metal belt buckles were forbidden, and work clothes had to be pocketless to make sure no one was carrying objects that could rub together and create a spark. And no one was allowed to have wooden matches at work or in their homes.

As safely as they could, the DuPont Company turned out millions of pounds of black powder and explosives that were put to use in World War I, in World War II, and in the blasting projects that created the Grand Coulee Dam, the Alaska Railroad, and the Panama Canal.

The plant shut down in 1976, sixty-seven years after it opened, and today the company town's original butcher shop serves as the home of the DuPont Historical Museum. That's where you can see all sorts of photos and memorabilia about the making of dynamite and the inevitable explosions that occurred on-site, as well as a machine once used to mix and press dynamite into sticks. You'll also see examples of the special tools used at the plant, such as wooden shovels and non-sparking welding torches.

The DuPont Historical Museum is located at 207 Barksdale Avenue in Dupont. From Interstate 5, take exit 119 and follow it to Barksdale Avenue, which is Dupont's main street. For more information phone (253) 964-2399 or visit www.dupontmuseum.com.

He Just Keeps Rolling Along
Edmonds

In the late 1960s Bobj Berger (he added the "j" to distinguish himself from other Bobs and pronounces his name "Bob-Jay") and a friend each agreed to start toilet paper collections. "We'd bring home two rolls from wherever we went," recalls Berger. "My friend moved away, but I just kept going."

The first item in Berger's collection was a bright pink roll of toilet paper with French writing on one side and English script on the other.

A shrine on the throne for The Duke.

Then his sister brought him samples snitched from both first- and tourist-class restrooms on a train trip in Germany. Soon toilet paper was rolling in from all over the world. Berger has fuchsia-colored toilet paper from Bali that is the consistency of crepe paper, a wrapped roll from a Martinique Club Med bathroom with the brand name "Dou Dou" printed on it, and a Swedish brand called Edet Kräpp. "I don't even know the color and consistency of some of these rolls," says Berger, "because I just can't bear to take off the wrapper."

Berger's toilet paper collection now numbers around 200 rolls and includes examples of politics-inspired paper bearing the names of Ronald Reagan, George Bush, Lyndon Johnson, and other former presidents, and a few movie stars, including a John Wayne brand that bears the slogan, "It's rough, it's tough and it don't take crap off nobody."

There's one special roll of "regionally significant" toilet paper that Berger considers his ultimate find. It's a roll of MD brand paper, with a green cross and the face of a nurse imprinted on the wrapper. Introduced by the Georgia-Pacific Company in the 1930s, it was reportedly the subject of a lawsuit brought by both the American Medical Association and the Red Cross. Berger believes he has the actual roll displayed as evidence when the toilet paper was ordered to appear in court. Plans are under way for the construction of special display shelves in a building adjacent to Berger's main house.

"The shelves will have to be covered in Plexiglas," says Berger, "so I don't lose any rare rolls." That's happened: An old roommate, confronted with the cardboard end of a roll, just couldn't resist the temptation to break into Berger's stash of pink French-Canadian privy paper that had French writing on one side and English on the other. That roommate was soon flushed from the house.

Bobj Berger offers tours of his toilet paper collection by appointment only. For information call (425) 774-9165.

Round Rocks and Roosterettes

Gig Harbor

In 1935 Gig Harbor resident and consummate showman Clarence East Shaw created two of the town's most memorable and unusual traditions.

The first was rooster racing. From 1935 until 1948 Shaw staged races in which a half dozen specially trained roosters ran down an 80-yard track. Shaw's first fleet-footed fowl foray, though, involved chickens. According to newspaper reports, the first "rooster" race pitted Dot and Dash, two chickens, against each other. Dot emerged victorious, running 80 yards in 18.5 seconds.

Rooster racing got to be so popular in Gig Harbor that Shaw created Roosterville, a miniature town filled with tiny buildings that sported farm-inspired names such as the Sit and Hatch Grocery, the Bill Comb Barbershop, and the Scratch and Mash Garage. Attendants at the attraction were local girls, called Roosterettes, whose on-duty uniforms were short majorette-style outfits with rooster comb hats.

So what could top rooster racing? Shaw's Round Rock contest, of course. Each year, Shaw offered cash prizes for the five rocks or stones judged to be the most perfectly rounded. Qualifying stones had to come from Washington State and be naturally round. No scratching or shaping was allowed.

If you want to know who won, stop by the Gig Harbor Peninsula Historical Society Museum, where some of the winning rocks are on display. Think you have a competition-worthy rock in your collection? The museum recently revived the Round Rock contest, and winning rocks are displayed each June, during the area's Maritime Gig Festival.

Of course, there's more to see at this museum than just those round rocks and some photos of racing roosters. The museum has a changing exhibition gallery, plenty of historical exhibits, and a wide variety of entertaining ephemera that includes the printed rules for the rock contest and a curious invitation to an early ball game that pitted the area's "fat ladies against the lean ladies."

The Gig Harbor Peninsula Historical Society and Museum is located at 4218 Harborview Drive in Gig Harbor. For hours and directions call (253) 858-6722 or check the museum's Web site, www.gigharbor museum.org.

Gig Harbor's Roosterettes made sure rooster races didn't run afoul.

CLAMS FROM OUTER SPACE?

Spend any time along the Washington coast or Puget Sound and you'll hear tales of geoducks (pronounced gooey-ducks). Now these creatures aren't ducks at all, but a species of large saltwater clams (*Panopea generosa*) that is native to the Pacific Northwest and most abundant in southern Puget Sound.

Geoducks aren't just big clams. They're huge. In fact, geoducks are the largest burrowing bivalves in the world and the largest clams in North America. How big? Well, geoducks average between one and three pounds, and there are plenty of specimens that have weighed in at up to twelve pounds. There have even been tales of geoducks that have topped the scales at thirty-five pounds.

Seeing a geoduck for the first time, at a seafood store or, perhaps, dug up by someone at the beach, can be a shocking sight. Geoduck shells can grow to about a foot long, and their wrinkled siphon, or foot (which reminds many people of a certain part of the male anatomy), can reach 2 or 3 feet in length. These creatures are also quite hardy: Although they stop growing when they're about twenty years old, geoducks can live up to 140 years.

Geoducks are also crafty. Excellent diggers, they're exposed only a few hours a month when the tides are extremely low. But even then, getting any of these giant clams out of the sand is quite a chore. The hunt seems to be worth the effort, though. Considered a delicacy in Asian countries along the Pacific and in Taiwan, they fetch a hefty price.

Giant Gopher Holes?

Tumwater

They look awfully strange and sort of funny: thousands of grassy lumps, each from 5 to 7 feet tall, spread out across 445 acres near Olympia. Officially they're called Mima Mounds, and they're classified as a type of ground pattern that contains organized, regularly spaced mounds. Similar bumpy fields have been discovered in Africa, South America, Wyoming, and California, but no one knows for sure how any of these mound fields were created.

There are plenty of theories, though, some likely, some pretty far out. Early explorers who trekked through the Northwest thought that perhaps the hills were Native American burial mounds. They were wrong. Scientific (and not-so-scientific) papers have hypothesized that the mounds were created by frost heaves, retreating glaciers, earthquakes, vortices, millions of ants, or giant prehistoric gophers. Could be.

In the past the area around the mounds was kept cleared. These days, moss, ferns, and the surrounding forest are creeping up and over many of the mounds. Now a registered natural landmark, the Mima Mounds Natural Area Preserve is open to the public. The site offers hiking trails that lead through prairie and forest areas, and informational panels describing some of the "creation" theories. Maybe you'll figure out the mystery.

The Mima Mounds Natural Area Preserve is open year-round. To get to the mounds, take I-5 to exit 95 (at Littlerock) and take Maytown Road about 4 miles to Littlerock. Turn right on Waddell Creek Road. The park is less than a mile down this road. For more information and directions call the Washington Department of Natural Resources at (360) 902-1340.

Try Flying This
Mukilteo

Who hasn't taken a piece of scrap paper, folded it up into a paper air-plane, and sent it flying across the room or out the window? The folks at the Dillon Works! company in Mukilteo probably do this on a regular basis as they sit at their desks trying to think up creative designs for the imaginative "dimensional elements" they fabricate for theme parks, casi-nos, restaurants, trade show exhibitors, and other clients nationwide.

The company's dimensional elements run the gamut from giant pan-cakes and outsize candies to animal eyeballs and towering company mascots. So with a tip of the wing to a serious business that's often

Office daydreaming led to this giant one-ton "paper" airplane.

filled with fun and, at times, irreverence, the folks at Dillon Works! created a 26-foot "paper" airplane and then had it set on top of their company's headquarters. The plane, which appears to have simply sailed onto the company's roof, serves as an awning over the front door.

Although this aircraft weighs more than a ton and is made from a steel frame covered with yellow fiberglass, it looks as if it's made from a single sheet of ruled yellow legal paper, complete with red and blue lines and a crumpled front nose.

You can see what some people call the world's largest paper airplane at Dillon Works! at 11775 Harbor Reach Drive in Mukilteo. For more information call (425) 493-8309 or log on to www.dillonworks .com.

Does It Have Its Own Weather?

Mukilteo

Before the Puget Sound area was known for coffee and software, it was famous for being the home of the bustling aircraft plants owned by the Boeing Company. Still, in 1966, when the company announced it was going to start building 747s, then the world's largest jet airliners, the big question in town was: *Where?*

The answer: inside the world's largest building, of course, which the company then proceeded to build on a swath of land 30 miles north of Seattle. Locals and out-of-towners alike were so curious about the building and about how the massive airplanes were being put together that tours of the plant started as soon as the first 747 was completed. In the first year fewer than 40,000 people stopped by, but now almost 200,000 people take the tour each year, making the Boeing factory one of the state's most popular tourist attractions.

These days, the *Guinness Book of World Records* lists Boeing's plant as the largest building in the world by volume. Few would argue: The eleven-story structure encompasses 472 million cubic feet of space and covers more than ninety-eight acres. Giant 747s, 767s, 777s, and the new 787s can be built here at a rate of up to five per month.

Want a firsthand look at doors as large as football fields and the 31 miles of track needed for the more than two dozen overhead cranes? One-hour tours, which include a series of short films and a tour of the plant, are offered several times each weekday until midafternoon. Before you head out there, though, there are some basic ground rules: no kids less than 4 feet 2 inches tall; no babes in arms; and no hand-held items such as purses, cameras, binoculars, or cell phones. Be ready for some walking (about a third of a mile) and for a climb up some steep stairs.

The tours are impressive, but so are the exhibits next door at the Future of Flight Museum, which opened in 2005. In addition to a wide variety of hands-on displays and an XJ5 flight simulator, visitors can design their own airplanes—from engine to paint job—and get a free printout of their creations. Those truly fond of their flying machines can even arrange to have their designs transferred to a T-shirt to wear home.

The Future of Flight Aviation Center and the Boeing Tour are located at 8415 Paine Field Boulevard in Mukilteo, about 30 miles north of Seattle via I-5. It's a good idea to make reservations and purchase tickets ahead of time, especially around the holidays and during the summer. For directions and more information call (888) 467-4777 or visit www .futureofflight.org.

Tiffany's Last Commission
Olympia

While schoolkids and fans of the political process everywhere make it a point to visit their state capitol to see legislators in action, visiting Washington State's Legislative Building offers a few added attractions for fans of art, architecture, and symbolism.

Built in 1928, the domed building sits on a bluff overlooking Puget Sound and looks very much like the U.S. Capitol in Washington, D.C.

Lots to see inside the Capitol building.

Besides the dome, the building's other most notable feature is the chandelier in the rotunda. The five-ton Angels of Mercy chandelier, which hangs from the dome on a one-ton, 101-foot chain, was designed by Louis Comfort Tiffany as one of his last major commissions. Tiffany also designed the floor lamps, sconces, and many of the other chandeliers in the building.

The special touches don't end there. To symbolize Washington's place as the forty-second state in the Union, there are exactly forty-two granite steps leading up to the entrance of the building. The six huge bronze front doors, which weigh two tons each, are 15 feet tall and 4 inches thick. Images on the doors depict oxen pulling logs, Snoqualmie Falls, a sailing vessel, and assorted pioneer industries. In addition, each legislative chamber has elaborate plaster ceilings studded with eagles and gilded rosettes. If you look closely, you'll notice that the railings and even the doorknobs bear the official state seal.

The Legislative Building sustained a considerable amount of damage during the 6.8-magnitude Nisqually earthquake, which hit western Washington on February 28, 2001, at 10:54 a.m. Fortunately, though, $100 million had already been budgeted for renovation, which is happily completed. Now visitors can safely tour the Legislative Building as well as the Temple of Justice, where the state's supreme court does its business, the Governor's Mansion, and other buildings and memorials on the Capitol Campus, including the Capitol Conservatory, which is home to more than 500 varieties of tropical and desert plants.

To reach the Olympia Capitol Campus, take I-5 to exit 105 (heading south from Seattle) or exit 105A (heading north from Olympia and points south) and follow the signs to the campus. For more information call the State Capitol Visitor Center at (360) 664-3799 or visit www.ga .wa.gov/visitor/index.html.

A Pot to Sing In

Tacoma

At one time South Tacoma Way sported a bevy of unusual buildings. There were a few castle-shaped structures, a restaurant the color and shape of a lemon, a service station that looked just like a giant gasoline pump (complete with giant flowerpot-shaped restrooms labeled "Mom" and "Pop"), and a 25-foot-high coffeepot-shaped restaurant called, appropriately enough, the Coffee Pot Restaurant.

Only the coffeepot, now called Bob's Java Jive, has survived. Over the years it's had several makeovers, but it perseveres as a fun and funky destination for drinks, karaoke, blues, dancing, and live music.

Once the Coffee Pot Restaurant, this perky spot is now a bar.

Built in sections that were then trucked here and bolted together, the pot originally had outhouse restrooms in the shape of salt-and-pepper shakers. Later, in its most perky days, the pot's inside was decorated in a high Polynesian theme. A popular Jungle Room in back was presided over by two resident monkeys named Java and Jive, who were well known for their drum playing. At the urging of the health department, the monkeys retired, and today's decor is a bit more, well, eclectic. Or as one regular has cautiously and politely termed it, "divelike, but lovable."

Legend has it that the Ventures, of "Walk Don't Run" and "Telstar" fame, used to appear at Java Jive during the late 1950s on a regular basis, but never received more than $50 for an evening's gig.

The Java Jive is located at 2101 South Tacoma Way in Tacoma. For hours and entertainment schedule call (253) 475-9843.

Acres of Autos

Tacoma

By all accounts, Harold LeMay was a smart, hardworking, big-hearted fellow whose idle was set on high. A garbage collector by trade, LeMay built both the state's largest private refuse hauling company and what the *Guinness Book of World Records* once categorized as the largest privately owned automobile collection in the world.

Topping out at more than 3,000 vintage vehicles, LeMay's collection included 300 Cadillacs, a 1928 Stutz fire truck, a 1948 Tucker 48 (one of only fifty-one ever built), a 1958 Chrysler dual Ghia once owned by actor Peter Lawford, four double-decker buses, Indian motorcycles, the 1947 DeSoto station wagon seen on the *Happy Days* television show, and a rare 1960 Amphica, an amphibious car fitted with propellers so it could be "driven" in the water. He stored his treasures at his home and in more than fifty buildings throughout the area, and each year he'd hold an auto show and an open house that was attended by up to 10,000 people.

LeMay died in 2000 at age eighty-one, but the car show is still held each year on the last Saturday in August. Plans for the Harold E. LeMay Museum keep motoring along as well. Scheduled to open in 2009 on a nine-acre site next to the Tacoma Dome, which sits appropriately enough alongside I-5 in Tacoma, the museum will have viewable storage for up to 2,000 vintage cars, an experimental wind tunnel, and an eight-story double helix exhibit tower showcasing 150 of the finest cars in the collection.

Luckily there's no need to drive around aimlessly waiting for the official museum to open. Two-hour, 350-car guided tours of the collection are offered Tuesday through Saturday at 325 152nd Street East in the Spanaway-Parkland area of Tacoma. For appointments, admission costs, directions, and more information, call (253) 536-2885 or (877) 902-8490 or visit www.lemaymuseum .org.

A hopped-up Ford 32 Jet Car.

Galloping Gertie

Tacoma

Washington may have four of the world's eight floating highway bridges, but the most notorious bridge in the state is one that fell down.

On July 1, 1940, the 5,939-foot-long Tacoma Narrows Bridge opened to traffic. This man-made wonder had towers that reached 500 feet above the water and, at the time, was the third-longest suspension bridge in the world. More than just a great sight to behold, the bridge spanning the windy Tacoma Narrows created both a vehicular and economic link between the city of Tacoma and towns on the Olympic and Kitsap Peninsulas that had been isolated for generations.

Even before the bridge opened, though, trouble was brewing. During construction, workmen ate lemons to battle the seasickness they experienced when the bridge swayed. The rolling motion of the bridge prompted locals to dub it "Galloping Gertie," and on windy days many drivers gladly paid their tolls just to experience the sensation of seeing cars up ahead disappear in the "dips."

Galloping Gertie gave her last thrill ride on November 7, 1940, just four months after the gala opening. On that morning, the center span had been undulating 3 to 5 feet in winds of 35 to 46 miles per hour, and state police closed the bridge to traffic at 10:00 a.m. It soon stopped undulating and began twisting. The twisting grew so strong that the bridge started breaking apart and dropping, chunk by chunk, into the waters below. By 11:00 a.m. the entire bridge was gone. The only casualty was Tubby, a cocker spaniel whose owner had abandoned his car midspan and crawled to safety.

Galloping Gertie was replaced with another much safer bridge, which some called "Sturdy Gertie," about ten years later. The new bridge is 40 feet longer than the original Gertie, whose sunken remains qualify as the largest man-made structure ever lost at sea and are now on the National Register of Historic Places.

The new Narrows Bridge, which is part of State Route 16, now has a companion. A suspension bridge, which opened to traffic in Summer 2007, was built parallel to and south of the existing bridge to ease traffic congestion between Tacoma and Kitsap Peninsula. By summer 2008 both bridges will be open to motorists—the old bridge serving westbound traffic and the new bridge carrying eastbound traffic.

When Galloping Gertie collapsed, the bridge was replaced by Sturdy Gertie.

Historic Doodles and Documents

Tacoma

Although some libraries have a room where they keep rare books and documents, most libraries are filled with standard-issue printed volumes of text. The Karpeles Manuscript Library in Tacoma, however, has fifty oak-and-glass cases reserved for the display of original documents penned by notable authors, scientists, statesmen, artists, and other people who had something to say and who took the time to write it out by hand.

The library collection began in the late 1970s, when David Karpeles started attending auctions and buying original manuscripts. He picked up a copy of the Emancipation Proclamation signed by Abraham Lincoln, Benjamin Franklin's "taxation without representation" letter to King George III, and Mozart's score for the *Marriage of Figaro*. The false starts, new directions, doodlings, and crossed-out words on what have turned out to be important primary historical documents, Karpeles realized, offered clues to the thinking behind great deeds and works of art and helped turn history into a lively and fascinating subject.

The Karpeles Manuscript Collection now hovers around a million documents, and rather than keep them in a private reading room, the Karpeles family parcels out portions of the collection among the eight branches of the museum that are scattered around the country, including the Karpeles Manuscript Museum in Tacoma. Although the Tacoma branch has a few Northwest-related documents that stay here permanently, most documents in the collection stay at manuscript headquarters in Santa Barbara, where themed exhibits are prepared and sent off around the country for three-month stints at the branches. Each exhibit is centered on a particular individual, historical event, or aspect of society. For example, past exhibits in Tacoma have featured Thomas Edison's letters, original music manuscripts, documents relating to the

Civil War, and the scientific papers of Charles Darwin.

The museum building, with its six large Greco-Roman columns, faces Wright Park and is just across the street from the 1908 W. W. Seymour Botanical Conservatory, one of only three such Victorian greenhouses on the West Coast. The Karpeles Manuscript Library Museum is located at 407 South G Street in Tacoma. Phone (253) 383-2575 or visit www .rain.org/~karpeles for more information.

Blessed Beans
Vashon Island

Nationwide, there are monasteries doing a brisk mail-order business in everything from religious items and smoked cheese to fudge, bourbon balls, and cheesecake. And while the chief work of the two monks at the Russian Orthodox Holy Brotherhood of the Monastery of the All-Merciful Saviour on Vashon Island is that of prayer, they also grow as much of their own food as they can and earn cash from selling their gourmet line of Monastery Blend Coffees and Orthodox Monk Teas.

The coffee business started back in the early 1990s when a church supporter who's also a Seattle-based specialty coffee roaster learned of Father Tryphon's devotion to a good cup of morning coffee. The roaster offered to work with Father Tryphon to develop a few gourmet coffee blends that the monastery could sell under its own private label. They eventually brewed up blends with names such as Abbot's Choice, Promised Blend, and Deacon's Decaf, and now sell the coffee at several local markets and bookstores, and nationwide via their Web site.

At first the monks marketed their coffee with the slogan, "To Drink Any Other Coffee Would Be a Sin," but they decided to drop that wording after receiving some complaints from people who thought they were making fun of sin. Even without that slogan, the Monastery Blend

Coffee business has been quite successful. So successful, in fact, that for a while the monks had to wage a legal battle with Starbucks over a Christmas Blend. The giant coffee company's lawyers claimed that Starbucks had trademarked the term, but the monks prevailed and continue to offer the seasonal blend along with other big sellers such as Byzantium, a Greek-style coffee that is ground to a fine powder.

The All-Merciful Saviour Russian Orthodox Monastery on Vashon Island welcomes visitors, but requests that you call ahead (206-463-3461) in order to honor the solitude of the monks. You can learn more about the monastery and order coffee from www.vashonmonks.com.

Bicycle-Eating Tree
Vashon Island

Although it's a fast fifteen-minute ferry ride from West Seattle or Tacoma to Vashon Island, slow-going is the rule once you arrive. For example, the sign over the counter at the Malt Shop near downtown Vashon suggests that if you're in a hurry, "come back when you're not."

So perhaps it's not such a stretch to imagine that years ago a youngster might have propped a bicycle up against a tree thinking he'd come back for it when he wasn't so busy exploring curious things in the woods. And maybe he found something so delightful he ran home to show it to the family. And then

On Vashon Island, bicycles grow on trees.

maybe he just forgot about that bicycle propped up against the tree.

For a very long time.

Or maybe not. But somehow, sometime, someone left a bicycle leaning against a certain tree for so long that the tree grew up around the bike. Today the handlebars and the front wheels of this long-forgotten bicycle are gone, but you can still clearly see the frame and the rear wheel embedded in the trunk.

To see the Vashon Bike Tree, drive or bike from the ferry dock through downtown Vashon and park near Sound Food, which is on the left-hand side of the road near the intersection of SW 204th Street. There's a pathway to the left of the building that leads to the Bike Tree, just a few yards into the woods.

Bunk Down the (Sort of) Western Way

Vashon Island

As a kid growing up in eastern Washington, Judith Mulhair loved playing Cowboys and Indians. As an adult, she fell in love with world travel, first as a flight attendant and then as a cultural guide for her sons, Jake and Dirk.

The family so enjoyed the experience of staying at youth hostels, which are low-cost, dormitory-style lodgings where travelers share meals and chores, that when they got back to the States, Mulhair decided to turn her ten-acre ranch on Vashon Island into a hostel as well. Instead of the usual dormitories, though, Mulhair adopted a Wild West theme. That means that travelers at this official American Youth Hostel site have their choice of sleeping in a tepee, in a covered wagon, in the log bunkhouse, or in their own tents out in the field. Each evening there's a campfire to gather around, and each morning everyone is invited to the make-your-own pancake breakfast.

It's a great deal of fun and quite an inexpensive way to travel. That is, if you don't mind rustic sleeping and bathing arrangements, and if you don't get too concerned about historical accuracy. Tepees are the sort of housing that would have been found on the Plains back east, or in the movies. The Kwakiutl and other Pacific Northwest tribes were more likely to live in red cedar bark lodges.

The AYH Ranch is open May 1 through October 31. To get there from the ferry dock, follow Vashon Highway and turn right on Cove Road (look for the sign with the tepee). The ranch is about 1.5 miles farther on your left. For more information call (206) 463-2592 or check the hostel's Web site, www.vashonhostel.com.

Hostelers choose between tepees and covered wagons at the AYH Ranch.

OLYMPIC PENINSULA AND COAST

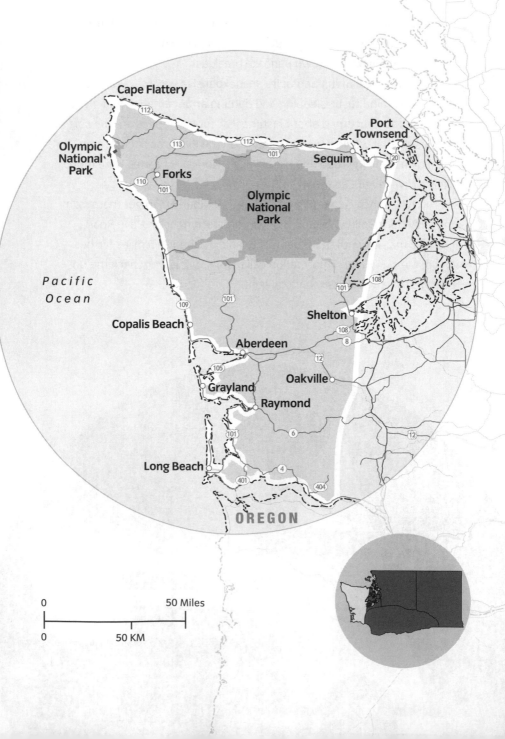

Cape Flattery

Olympic National Park

Forks

Olympic National Park

Port Townsend

Sequim

Pacific Ocean

Copalis Beach

Shelton

Aberdeen

Oakville

Grayland

Raymond

Long Beach

OREGON

0   50 Miles

0   50 KM

OLYMPIC PENINSULA
and Coast

The Olympic Peninsula and the Pacific Coast reflect perfectly the yin and yang of Washington. In general, beach communities along the 157 miles of coastline maintain a low-key demeanor year-round, but at least one town on the Long Beach Peninsula (home to the longest natural beach in the United States) does its best to beckon tourists with some classic roadside attractions, including a giant frying pan, a huge squirting razor clam, and a mysterious "alligator man" that P. T. Barnum would be proud of.

This region of the state is also filled with extremes. In the rain forest you'll find some of the tallest trees, biggest slugs, and highest annual rainfall in the continental United States. Yet the communities around Sequim and the Dungeness Valley boast about how little rain they get. Perhaps that's why soggy Forks hosts a Rainfest each year while sunny Sequim has an annual festival that honors the pioneers who brought with them the concept of irrigation.

Concrete Cobain

Aberdeen

Folks in the struggling logging community of Aberdeen have some mixed feelings about Kurt Cobain. For a while he was a local kid who made good. His grunge band, Nirvana, sold millions of records, and he was an international celebrity. Unfortunately, Cobain was also a drug addict who killed himself in 1994, leaving a suicide note that ended, "So remember, it's better to burn out than to fade away."

While debates swirled about where Cobain's ashes would be scattered, music fans worldwide mourned the singer with poems and song. One Aberdeen woman turned her sadness into a giant work of art. In the corner of her family's downtown muffler shop, sculptor Randi Hubbard created a 600-pound concrete statue of Kurt Cobain. *All Apologies,* which takes its title from a Nirvana song, shows an unshaven Cobain playing the guitar with a tear rolling down his face.

Hubbard had hoped to put the statue in one of Aberdeen's public parks, but when folks started arguing about whether or not it was appropriate to do so, the city council suggested that Hubbard find another spot for her artwork. So until a permanent home can be found for the statue, it remains in the muffler shop, in its own separate room complete with records, photographs, Nirvana-related memorabilia, and several other Hubbard sculptures.

Hubbs Muffler is at 2208 Sumner Avenue in Aberdeen. The shop is usually open Monday through Saturday, but for exact hours and directions call (360) 533-1957.

While in town, Nirvana fans should be sure to stop by the Aberdeen Museum of History at 111 East Third Street to pick up a copy of the self-guided walking tour of Kurt Cobain's Aberdeen. The tour, which is also on the museum's Web site, includes stops at many of the homes, schools, and businesses where Cobain lived, spent time, trespassed, and practiced music. For more information contact the Aberdeen Museum of History at (360) 533-1976 or visit www.aberdeen-museum.org/kurt.htm.

Aberdeen is about 100 miles southwest of Seattle. From Interstate 5, head west on U.S. Highway 101, then continue west on State Route 8 and U.S. Highway 12.

The End of the Road
Cape Flattery

In this book full of firsts, biggests, and oldests, we offer Cape Flattery as a "most." Located on the tip of the Olympic Peninsula, on the Makah Indian reservation, Cape Flattery is the most northwestern point in the contiguous United States. It's certainly nice to know it's there, but it's even nicer to go there, because anyone who does says the views are most rewarding.

British captain James Cooke named this spot Cape Flattery in 1778, saying that the point of land "flattered us with the hopes of finding a harbour." To truly enjoy the views he encountered, you'll need to find the Cape Flattery Trail. That entails driving as far as you can on State Route 112, finding the Makah Tribal Center, and then subjecting your car's finish to 4 miles of gravel road. But anyone who's made the trek will tell you that the breathtaking views of the Pacific Coast offered along the hiking trail are most spectacular, especially now that the Makahs have renovated the trail, which for many years was so muddy and poorly maintained that hikers felt in danger of plunging over the cliffs.

Today, though, thanks to grants from both the Department of Natural Resources and the State Department of Transportation and the construction skills of tribe members, the trail is a delight to behold. The new and improved ¾-mile trail has a cedar boardwalk, stone and gravel steps with handrails, and four observation decks offering great views of the Pacific Ocean, the Strait of Juan de Fuca, Vancouver, and Tatoosh Island, a former Makah fishing and whaling camp later used as a Coast Guard station.

For more information and specific driving directions, visit www.north olympic.com/capeflatterytrail/.

Low-Tide Landing
Copalis Beach

With 28 miles of hard sand, Washington's Long Beach Peninsula boasts that it has the world's longest drivable beach. And while racing your buggy on a beach may have its attractions, consider the thrill and the challenge of landing your airplane on a beach, especially if that runway disappears twice each day.

Copalis Beach Airport, at the mouth of the Copalis River, is the only known beach airport in the United States and the only stretch of beach

Now you see the runway, now you don't.

in Washington State where it's legal to land an airplane. Open year-round, this airport has some unusual characteristics. On the upside, the clam digging is excellent and the views of the Pacific Ocean are divine. On the downside, though, the runway and the airplane parking lot are underwater during high tides. And pilots who do attempt to set down here must make sure not to land on any of the animals, vehicles, or pedestrians that also have legal access to the beach. Of course, when the tides recede, pilots must watch out for driftwood and other debris left behind.

Those challenges don't seem to be too much of a deterrent. In fact, on busy weekends there's one more obstacle pilots must watch out for: other airplanes. According to the Washington State Department of Transportation (WSDOT), "as many as 75 aircraft have been reported as being parked there at one time."

Inaccessible from the road and unusable at high tide, the Copalis Beach Airport is on State Route 109 at Copalis Beach. For more information visit www.wsdot.wa.gov/aviation/Airports/Copalis.htm.

Was That the Talkie-Tooter I Heard?

Forks

The community of Forks, located in the heart of the Olympic Peninsula's "West End," is surrounded by forests and filled with folks who are so darned proud of the town's timber heritage that the local high school carpentry class joined forces with inmates from the Olympic Correction Center to build the town a Timber Museum. Out of wood, of course.

Outside the building there's a fire lookout tower and the Forks Logger's Memorial. Inside the two-story structure are all sorts of saws and other logging equipment, a full-scale bunkhouse, a 9-foot stove from a logging camp cookhouse, and information about forest fires. Of special interest is the large wall plaque, designed by Keith Hoofnagle, which serves as a dictionary of logging terms. For example, a "talkie-tooter" is the radio whistle used to give signals. A "catface" is a partially healed fire scar on a tree. A "monthly insult" was what loggers called their pay-checks, but it seems that never stopped them from celebrating "alibi day," or payday, by developing "toothaches" or some other malady that required them to make a trip into town.

To learn more logger lingo, visit the Forks Timber Museum on 1421 South Forks Avenue, at the south end of town. Just look for the large wooden *Buckers* sculpture that stands outside the museum. The carv-ing was made by noted local chain saw artist Dennis Chastain. For hours and information phone (360) 374-9663 or see www.forks-web .com/fg/timbermuseum.htm.

All manner of woods-wisdom is dispensed at the Forks Timber Museum.

IRON MAN OF THE HOH

In 1885 German immigrant John Huelsdonk homesteaded on a swatch of forest land in the Hoh River Valley, about 27 miles south of what is now the town of Forks. He insisted that his four daughters attend college, and he worked on his land right up until his death in 1945 at age seventy-nine.

Those are fine accomplishments on their own, but that's not why folks in town still marvel about Huelsdonk. This strong and determined man became known as the Iron Man of the Hoh for a variety of feats that he may or may not have accomplished, but they are certainly inspiring

For example, Huelsdonk supposedly killed more than 150 cougars during his lifetime in the woods, and when he worked as a logger, he'd regularly hike through 70 miles of forest paths in order to be with his family each weekend.

The story that's gained Huelsdonk Paul Bunyan–like status, however, tells about the time a friend came upon Huelsdonk on a forest trail with a cookstove strapped to his back. "Isn't that stove heavy?" the friend asked. "Nah, the stove's not heavy," Huelsdonk supposedly replied, "just the fifty-pound sack of flour in the oven."

SLUGS

You'll encounter slugs pretty much anywhere you go in wet western Washington. These oozy, slimy, prehistoric-looking mollusks appear to be snails that have left their shells behind. The uninitiated might think someone's been doling out 3- to 5-inch blobs of green, black, or brown toothpaste.

You'll find slugs and their slimy trails in likely and unlikely places: in your garden, trailing across the sidewalk, hanging off the branch of a tree, or inching up the side of your house.

Slugs are gastropods, which means they are belly-footed and refers to the fact that they move along the ground on one foot. Of the many varieties of slugs that inch around the Northwest, the most well known is the banana slug, aptly named for its color: bright yellow, often mottled with brown spots. This creature is notorious because it can grow up to 10 inches long, weigh up to half a pound, and stretch to more than a foot in length when it's crawling along.

Want to know more?

• Slugs are hermaphrodites: Every slug has male and female reproductive systems.

• Slugs can stretch to twenty times their normal length and squeeze through tiny openings.

• Slugs are tough: They can crawl across brick, crushed glass, and razor blades without getting hurt.

- Slugs can follow slime trails that they left the night before.
- Slug eggs left in the soil can survive for years and hatch when conditions are right.
- There have been reports of some foot-long super slugs.
- Slug control often consists of a salt shaker (the salt "melts" the slug) or a pie tin full of beer. Slugs crawl in, get drunk, and drown.

The slow-moving banana slug can grow up to 10 inches long and weigh up to half a pound.

Look Up—And Don't Forget Your Slicker

Forks

Head to the Olympic National Forest on the Olympic Peninsula, and you'll encounter just one stoplight on a scenic 160-mile stretch of US 101. That will be in the town of Forks, and as long as you have to stop for that red light, you might as well get out of your car and visit.

Whether you hang around to eat, shop, or find out about all the likely spots to go fishing, it's a good chance it will be raining. That's because the average annual rainfall in Forks is between 120 and 140 inches. That's not counting the fog or the 11 inches of snowfall that accumulate each year.

Think that's bad? In 1997 Forks received 162.14 inches of rain, breaking a record set back in 1921. What did the Forks folk do then? They celebrated! They made a special T-shirt, and a local folksinger wrote a song to commemorate the event. The song was a big hit at the town's annual Rainfest.

As a result of all that rain, at least one of the record-size trees on the American Forest Association's list of "largest living specimens" is nearby. On your way to the Hoh Rain Forest Visitor Center, you can pull over—or just lean out the window—and marvel at a sitka spruce that is 191 feet tall and more than 707 inches around.

But wait, there's more: Within the boundaries of the Olympic National Park there are ten more record-setting trees, including a 241-foot-tall western hemlock and a 212-foot-tall Douglas fir. To learn more about the Olympic National Park and the rain forest, log on to www.npr.gov/olym or call (360) 565-3130 to get visitor information.

Pick or Pluck?

Grayland

Don't go thinking that cranberries are just a Cape Cod commodity. The tart red berries have been growing wild in Washington's coastal peat bogs since the end of the last ice age, and there are now miles of cultivated bogs reaching from the Long Beach Peninsula up toward Grayland

Until the 1940s cranberry picking was a really tough job. A picker would have to get down on hands and knees, pluck the berries, then put them into a big box. Later, one- and two-handed cranberry scoops helped ease the pickers' job, and in the early 1950s suction pickers made the harvest a bit smoother. But it was a creative cranberry farmer with a sore back who revolutionized cranberry picking forever.

When venturing out into a cranberry bog, be sure to wear the right shoes.

In 1956 Julius Furford applied his welding skills to the backbreaking work of cranberry picking and came up with an automated cranberry picker. His device was essentially a motorized machine with "combs" on the bottom that moved through fields, picking up the cranberry vines and plucking off the berries. In addition to plucking the berries, to the delight of cranberry farmers everywhere, the picker pruned the vines as well. "People had their doubts," remembers one local citizen, "but after watching him speed through his picking day, they were convinced."

Furford went on to build and sell hundreds of his patented picking machines to cranberry farmers around the world, and he continued working at his manufacturing plant until about six months before his death at age ninety-one. Now Furford's original automated cranberry picker and all manner of cranberry industry memorabilia are on display at the Furford Cranberry Museum. That's Furford himself narrating the video that shows cranberry pickers in action, both before and after the invention of the Furford Picker.

The Furford Cranberry Museum is located at 2395 State Route 105 in Grayland and is open by request. Call (360) 267-5403 to arrange a tour.

If you crave even more cranberry culture, head on down to Long Beach Peninsula, where there's a Cranberry Festival each October (National Cranberry Month). You can also stroll through a working bog and tour the exhibits at the Pacific Coast Cranberry Research Foundation at 2907 Pioneer Road in Long Beach. For more information phone (360) 642-5553 or visit www.cranberrymuseum.com.

Giant Pan for a Squirting Clam

Long Beach

In the early 1940s local officials in Long Beach were looking for an advertising gimmick that would be sure to lure tourists to the coastal community. Funds were tight, but everyone agreed that the campaign had to be big and it had to have sizzle.

The solution, a giant cast-iron frying pan, met the criteria on both counts. Introduced at the town's 1941 Razor Clam Festival, the 1,300-pound, 10-by-20-foot pan was used first to fry the largest razor clam fritter and then to fry up to 200 pounds of fritters at a time.

The pan was a huge hit, and for years after it was a featured attraction at festivals and fairs around the state. Today, those who want to gaze upon the giant pan must travel to downtown Long Beach, where it now hangs in a pocket park, right next to a giant razor clam that squirts faithfully each hour for

This 1,300-pound cast-iron frying pan once fried the world's largest razor clam fritter.

clam fans, pan fans, and folks in search of an old-style photo op.

Big as it is, Long Beach's frying pan has competition for the title of world's largest. The folks in Rose Hill, North Carolina, have a big pan too, but instead of frying clams, they use their pan to fry thousands of whole chickens each year during the North Carolina Poultry Jubilee.

The giant pan used to fry razor clams is located on State Route 103 in downtown Long Beach, next to the giant squirting clam.

Half Man, Half Gator, 100% Good-Natured Huckstering
Long Beach

No trip to the Long Beach Peninsula is complete (or, if you have kids, allowed) without a stop at Marsh's Free Museum, an intriguing shop filled with unusual and bizarre items such as shrunken heads, historical artifacts, and—oh, yeah—plenty of souvenir T-shirts, saltwater taffy, and other vacation trinkets.

Marsh's is famous, however, for all the doodads, gee-gaws, small appliances, animal oddities, and "what could that be?" stuff tacked to the ceiling, hung on the walls, and snuggled into any open spot on the floor. Tops among the strange sights is Jake the Alligator Man. Also the shop's mascot, Jake is supposedly half man and half alligator. To see this strange creature, you have to make your way to the back corner of the shop. Along the way, there's plenty to distract you, including baubles to buy, a coin-operated music box urging you to hear the warbling of the mechanical "imported French canary," the "Throne of Love" that promises to test your passion, and displays of early mousetraps, century-old valentines, and oodles of other stuff that elicits a "what's that!?" response over and over.

Toward the front of the shop, up above the souvenir racks, are shelves displaying a two-headed pig and other odd animals. The kitty that for years purred loudly and lounged lazily by the store's front register is now freeze-dried and part of that display. Store owners claim that not long after that first cat was "shelved," another startlingly similar-looking cat walked in the front door and plopped himself down by the register. One way or another, we suspect he'll be sticking around.

Marsh's Free Museum (and gift shop) is located on the main drag of downtown Long Beach, which is State Route 103. Look for the Wild West–looking building, its low porch strewn with carved wooden cowboys, rusty old farm equipment, and baffled-looking tourists. For more information phone (360) 642-2188 or visit www.marshsfreemuseum .com.

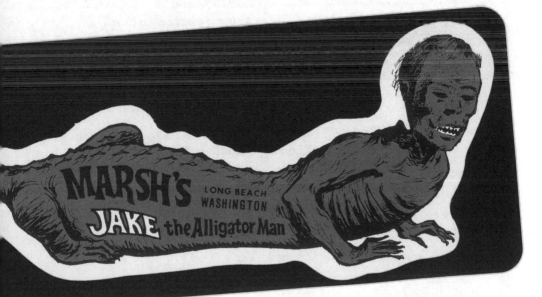

Is he a man? Is he an alligator?
He's Jake!

DOES IT TOP THE OTHERS?

Next time you go to the beach, look around for the gaggle of happy kids armed with pails, shovels, and the other simple tools needed to build sand castles that will certainly be washed away at high tide.

For some, this innocent childhood pastime has turned into a competitive adult sport. There are sand sculpture contests held up and down both coasts, and teams spend months designing and practicing in hopes of winning titles and prizes. Long Beach, for example, with one of the longest beaches in the world, has hosted an annual sand sculpture competition for more than eighteen years. Called SandStations, the event's cash prizes top out at $1,200.

Not to be outdone, the city of Port Angeles, known as the Gateway to Olympic National Park, has made its own bid for sand sculpture fame. As part of the 2002 Arts in Action Street Fair, a local castle-building team announced plans to build a record-breaking sand sculpture. After spending almost one hundred hours carefully piling and shaping 225 tons of sand, the team stepped back to admire a 29-foot-3½-inch-tall sand sculpture that looked like a cross between a melting ice-cream cone and a pine cone.

Before one grain of sand could be dislodged, an independent engineering firm stepped in to take measurements so proof of the sand sculpture could be forwarded to the folks at the *Guinness Book of World Records* for possible inclusion in their database. And the sculptor did indeed enter the record books. And just in time: Contest coordinators say that was the last year the *Guinness* folks included the tallest sand sculpture category.

Folks in Port Angeles make a bid for a spot in the sand sculpture records.

World's Biggest Burger
Long Beach

I don't know if it's actually the world's biggest burger, but I'm not sure I'd want to encounter one much bigger.

The Corral Drive-In offers up a giant Tsunami burger that starts with a five-pound patty on a 16-inch bun. Of course, if you're ordering something that big, you probably don't want it plain, so the burger comes topped with (are you ready?) sixteen slices of American cheese, a full cup of relish, two cups of mayonnaise, one and a half heads of lettuce, three tomatoes, and a goodly amount of mustard and pickles.

Bet you can't eat even one of these giant burgers.

Who eats these things? According to the folks behind the counter, the Tsunami usually gets cut into burger slices to feed a group of people. If you'd like to test out one of these megaburgers, be advised that you need to call in your order at least a day in advance. And be sure to bring along plenty of hungry friends. The Corral Drive-In is located at 2506 Pacific Avenue North in Long Beach; call (360) 642-2774.

MORE CURIOUS BURGERS

If you're not up for a giant Tsunami burger at the Corral Drive-In, some smaller but still somewhat unusual burgers are offered at other establishments on the Long Beach Peninsula.

Thursday is Burger Night at the Depot Restaurant and Tavern. Folks can order up to fifteen different toppings for their burgers, including fried eggs, avocado, jalapeños, and pineapple. The Depot is at 38th Street and L Place, Seaview; (360) 642-7880.

Not interested in beef? The 42nd Street Cafe offers oyster burgers (panfried oysters on a burger bun) at 4201 Pacific Way in Seaview; (360) 642-2323.

Let's Go Fly a Kite
Long Beach

Each August, hundreds of kite fliers and thousands of spectators show up at Long Beach, hoping for just enough wind to make the Washington State International Kite Festival another sky-high success. Events range from fighter-kite demonstrations and wind art displays to a "mass ascension" in which organizers try to break the western hemisphere record for the most kites in the sky at one time.

Long Beach is not only a great place to go fly kites, it's also the home of the World Kite Museum and Hall of Fame, a small building filled with kites of all sizes, shapes, colors, and purposes. The collection includes kite books, colorful photographs of kites in flight, and more than 1,500 kites representing more than two dozen countries and practically every

Ready for take-off.

state. Some kites are no bigger than a matchbox, others seem way too big for liftoff, and several elaborate handmade kites from China and Japan look too beautiful and fragile to throw into the sky.

The museum not only displays colorful modern-day kites, it tells the story of kites in history, from Benjamin Franklin's electricity experiment with a kite and a key in 1752 to the kites emblazoned with pictures of enemy airplanes that were used to train World War II gunners. During the same era, box kites, known as "Gibson Girl" kites, were also standard equipment on lifeboats—not to provide entertainment at sea, but to raise an aerial so rescue signals could be transmitted.

The Kite Museum's Hall of Fame honors famous kite fliers and kite inventors, including Arthur Batut, a French photographer who in the late 1880s became known as the father of aerophotography. Batut, the story goes, once noticed a butterfly float by with perfectly still wings. From this, he somehow got the notion to attach a camera to a kite so he could take photos from the air. How did Batut snap his shots once the kite and camera were aloft? According to museum notes, before the contraption lifted off, Batut simply lit a match to a wick; when the wick burned down—voilà!—the skycam was born.

The World Kite Museum is located at 303 Sid Snyder Drive on the Sid Snyder Drive Beach approach. For more information call (360) 642-4020 or log on to www.worldkitemuseum.com. The Washington State International Kite Festival is held each August. For more information check out www.kitefestival.com.

KITE CURIOSITIES

- The most kites flown in the sky at one time is 4,663 at Long Beach, Washington.

- The largest number of kites flown on a single line is 11,284. The record is held by a class of Japanese schoolchildren.

- The fastest recorded speed of a kite is over 120 miles per hour.

- The record for the highest single kite flown is 12,471 feet.

- The world record for the longest "kite fly" is 180 hours.

- Kite flying was banned in China during the Cultural Revolution; people found flying kites were sent to jail for up to three years and had their kites destroyed.

- There are seventy-eight rules in kite fighting in Thailand.

- Kite flying was banned in Japan in 1760 because too many people preferred kite flying to working.

- Approximately twelve people are killed each year in kiting accidents throughout the world.

- The smallest kite flown was 0.39 x 0.31 inches.

Courtesy of the World Kite Museum

Would You Like That in Small Bills?

Oakville

Oakville has been a rough-and-ready town ever since its logging heyday in the 1890s. The town's bank has been in operation since 1909, and it seems it's been the target of a fair number of robberies over the years. Rather than hide this history, town officials are darn proud of the fact that on July 5, in 1938, 1939, 1940, or 1941 (no one can say for sure), the Oakville State Bank was the last Washington State bank robbed by a gunman who escaped on horseback.

These days, the bank has better security. But that last-robbery-on-horseback distinction is celebrated during Oakville's annual Independence Day Parade and Rodeo with a wild competition they call "The Last Horseback Bank Robbery Reenactment."

To set the scene, grass sod is laid out on the street in front of the bank. Then masked volunteers on horseback compete to stage the best robbery and galloping getaway. Robberies using more modern transportation also take place, in honor of the holdups that occurred in the 1940s.

The take? Not depositors' hard-earned cash, thank goodness. There's been enough of that. These days the loot consists of prizes awarded after judges measure the applause generated by the more than 2,000 people who come to witness the event (and maybe just to make sure their accounts are safe).

Robbery reenactments are part of Oakville's annual Independence Day Parade and Rodeo, held each year on the first weekend in July. For more information call (360) 273-2702 or visit www.oakville-wa.org.

The Sound of Silence
Olympic National Park

Gordon Hempton is obsessed with sounds. The sounds you can hear and those you can't. Or shouldn't. And that's why he's decided to do what he can to protect a natural soundscape in Washington State. Or at least the one square inch of it.

Hempton has circled the globe in search of silent places where he can record natural sounds and says he settled in Joyce, Washington, because it's near the Hoh Rain Forest and the Olympic National Park, the place he considers "perhaps the most richly endowed natural soundscape anywhere."

On regular hikes into the park, Hempton searches for the quiet, calm-inducing sounds of the forest, sounds such as leaves dropping

Shhh!

and birds chirping. But more often than not what he hears are out-of-place sounds such as generators, boom boxes, and airplanes flying overhead. So in an effort to restore and maintain the park's natural silence, he followed an elk trail to a truly quiet spot deep in the forest, placed a specially chosen red rock at the site, and declared the spot to be "One Square Inch of Silence" and off limits to non-natural sounds.

He knows it seems curious to concern himself with just one square inch but says that by protecting the natural sound at this one square inch of woods, he can have an impact on the sound a thousand miles around and above it. So, armed with a decibel-measuring sound-level meter and the address of the Internet site that shows airplane flight paths, he documents when an airplane flies over "his" one square inch and sends the airline a note asking it to steer clear. Some airlines do. American, Hawaiian, and Alaska Airlines have all written back to say that at least they'll try.

Hikers who come upon the One Square Inch of Silence can send silent messages to Hempton and others by placing notes in the "Jar of Quiet Thoughts" that sits by the stone that marks the site. "None of the messages can be taken or repeated in print," says Hempton, "but I can tell you that they cover everything from the natural events noticed in silence to thoughts on the meaning of silence and the notice of at least one marriage proposal made at this spot."

The closest city to One Square Inch is Forks. From Forks, go south on US 101 for 12 miles, turn left on Upper Hoh Road, and drive 18.5 miles to the visitor center parking lot. One Square Inch is located about 3 miles (about a two-hour hike) from the visitor center above Tom Creek Meadows at Olympic National Park. The exact location is marked by a small, red-colored stone placed on top of a moss-covered log. For directions visit www.onesquareinch.org/files/osidir.pdf. For more information about Gordon Hempton's efforts to document and protect natural sounds, call (360) 928-0151 or visit www.onesquareinch.org.

Long-Lost Locomotive
Port Townsend

William Matheson is "darn proud" that he helped solve a mystery that had been vexing folks at Fort Worden for sixty-two years.

Between 1890 and 1910 three forts—Fort Casey on Whidbey Island, Fort Flagler on Marrostone Island, and Fort Worden in Port Townsend—were built as seacoast artillery defense stations to protect the harbors and waterways of Puget Sound.

Like much of the other equipment that was used to build these forts, a Dinky steam locomotive was ordered to be destroyed after it had served its purpose. Colonel Garland Whistler was given the task of disposing of this huge hunk of metal, but seemed unhappy at the offer of just $30 to turn it into scrap. Instead, he ordered his men to bury the locomotive in the sand. Whistler washed his hands of the mess, and years later a storage shed was built over the locomotive's burial site.

You'd think it would be hard to forget where such a big object had been buried, but that's exactly what happened.

Deactivated in 1953, Fort Worden was turned into a 446-acre park with restored Victorian officers' houses, barracks, artillery bunkers, and a conference center. All in all, it's a picturesque setting that even provided the scenic backdrop for the movie *An Officer and a Gentleman*. Folks visit the park all the time, and a great deal of attention is paid to keeping the grounds looking lovely.

So in 1973, when William Matheson and his grounds crew were asked to take down a little-used shed, they got right to work. "I was digging down to remove the foundation and I hit this metal object," remembers Matheson. "We dug a little deeper, and there was what turned out to be a piece of one of the wheels from the long-lost locomotive. We'd heard rumors about it for years, and here it was."

But why was the locomotive lying there with its wheels sticking up?

"What they'd done," says Matheson, "is dig a big hole along the side of the train tracks and then they just tipped the locomotive over. Obviously they hadn't dug the hole deep enough, so that's why the wheels stuck out a bit at the top."

Matheson says that after he told the park manager about his find, "My gosh, the people started gathering right away. It was quite an event." Eventually a contracting firm was hired to pull the Dinky locomotive out of the ground, and now the unearthed engine is being cleaned and restored for public display.

This time, park officials say they'll keep better records so they don't lose the locomotive again.

Fort Worden is located at 200 Battery Way in Port Townsend. Just follow Cherry Street from downtown. For more information phone (360) 344-4400 or visit http://fortworden.org.

Kinetic Sculpture Race
Port Townsend

For just about twenty years now, Port Townsend residents have ushered in the fall season with what local organizers modestly declare to be the state's "Premier Human-Powered Vehicle Event." This raucous but highly entertaining and ecologically friendly weekend features a kinetic sculpture race, which has a couple of straightforward rules:

1. The vehicle must be people-powered and be able to perform on land and in water.
2. The wackier the contraption the better.

Inspired by a similar contest that first took place on Mother's Day 1969 in Ferndale, California, Port Townsend's "road rally" sends contestants through a 9-mile course that includes sand, water, and mud. Vehicles range from simple one-person contraptions to very highly engineered multipassenger machinery that can reach lengths of more than 75 feet.

Race prizes are as unusual as the contestants and their contraptions, and no one is scolded for trying to bribe the judges. Most sought after is the Mediocrity Award, which is ceremoniously given to the entrant whose finish time comes closest to the average time of the fastest and slowest contestants. Other prizes are awarded for best engineering, best showmanship, and the vehicle that carries the most passengers.

The Kinetic Sculpture Race is only one part of a weekend full of funky festivities. The schedule includes a Saturday parade through town, after which all vehicles entered in the race are tested for two very important characteristics: braking ability and buoyancy. (That should tell you something about the race.) There's also a Saturday night Koronation Kostume Ball (the coordinators' kooky spelling).

Port Townsend turns its streets, sidewalks, and sand areas over to the Kinetic Sculpture Race each year on the first weekend in October. For more information about the "kineticnauts" and their "kontraption," and about Port Townsend, call (888) 365-6978 or visit www.ptkinetic race.org.

KING OF THE CREEPY-CRAWLIES

David George Gordon studied fish in college and later went on to write books about lovable animals such as bald eagles and orca whales. But then he began to feel sluggish and went a bit buggy.

That was a good thing. Gordon wanted to introduce the general public to the sort of animals only a scientist could love. So he started researching and writing about slugs, the slimy, slow-moving creatures that inch ever so slowly around Northwest gardens and forest floors.

After slugs he took on another Northwest oddity: geoducks. These giant clams, Gordon notes, can live for up to 160 years and are a delicacy in many cultures.

If you visit David Gordon, be prepared to be offered a snack made of bugs.

CONTINUED

Next it was cockroaches, for a book titled *The Complete Cock-roach.* "They're the insect most people love to hate," says Gordon. "There are 5,000 species of cockroaches, and only 200 are considered pests. So there's a lot to learn about these curious critters."

It was while researching cockroaches that Gordon started discovering recipes that included bugs in the list of ingredients. "Turns out a lot of bugs are quite tasty," says Gordon, "and can be good for you. Some bugs are good sources of protein, while dried centipedes, scorpions, and cockroaches can cure all sorts of ailments."

How does he know? Well, Gordon actually cooked up a wide variety of bugs and then tasted them all as he tested out the recipes for his *Eat-A-Bug Cookbook,* which has suggestions for how to cook crickets, grasshoppers, ants, worms, termites, cockroaches, and all manner of other creepy-crawly things. "You can prepare lots of insects just by baking them and then covering them with chocolate," says Gordon, but he also has recipes for using insects in salads, soups, main courses, and appetizers. "You should try my Chirpy Chex Party Mix, which is made with cricket nymphs."

So if David Gordon will eat bugs, is there anything he won't eat? Well, you'll never see liver and onions on the menu at his house, nor will Chiquita and Dole, his 6-inch-long pet banana slugs, ever make it onto the breakfast plate. Just don't be surprised if he invites you to dinner and you discover that there's a fly doing the backstroke in your soup.

David Gordon's Recipe for White Chocolate and Waxworm Cookies

½ cup (about 75) live waxworms

2¼ cups whole wheat flour

1 tsp. baking soda

1 tsp. salt

1 cup (2 sticks) butter

¾ cup granulated sugar

¾ cup brown sugar

1 tsp. vanilla extract

2 large eggs

1¾ cups white chocolate bits

Instructions:

Sort waxworms from their wood shavings or other packing material. Rinse with cold water, drain, and put them in a sealed container. Freeze for three hours.

Combine flour, baking soda, and salt. Set aside.

Beat butter, granulated sugar, brown sugar, and vanilla, beating until creamy. Add eggs, beating well, then gradually add flour mixture.

Stir in white chocolate bits and ⅙ of the waxworms.

Drop by rounded tablespoon onto lightly greased cookie sheets.

Press two of the remaining waxworms into the top of each rounded tablespoon of cookie dough.

Bake at 375 degrees F for ten to twelve minutes or until golden brown. Cool on wire racks.

Yield: two dozen 4-inch cookies.

Note: Waxworms aren't really worms. They're the caterpillars of greater wax moths (*Galleria mellonella*). In the wild, they feed on the wax of honeybees' combs, hence their name. You can purchase live waxworms in small cottage-cheese-like containers from bait and tackle shops or pet suppliers. Kept cool and dry, a container of wax-worms will last for about two weeks. Baked, these ½-inch-long deli-cacies taste like pistachio nuts.

(Courtesy of and copyright © 2003 by David George Gordon)

Shoemaker to the Clowns

Port Townsend

Maybe Alan Zerobnick was just born with shoelaces in his veins.

Zerobnick comes from a long string of Polish, Czechoslovakian, and Russian shoemakers, and despite the fact that he was urged to become anything but a shoemaker ("A doctor would be nice"), he ended up making shoes.

At age fourteen Zerobnick started selling shoes. Later he helped a friend make sandals, stepping up to moccasins and eventually to his own brand of conventional "lasted" footwear.

Alan Zerobnick once made shoes only a clown could love.

Along the way Zerobnick spent eight years making shoes for a most unconventional clientele. As "Shoemaker to the Clowns," Zerobnick crafted custom-made footwear for the likes of Ronald McDonald, Patch Adams, enrollees in the Ringling Brothers Clown College, and a variety of professional clowns.

It sounds like it must have been loads of laughs, but Zerobnick says making good-fitting clown shoes was serious business. "These people must be on their feet for long hours and they need to be able to run around without falling over their feet." That is, I suppose, unless they mean to. "A clown shoe is actually a shoe within a shoe," explains Zerobnick. "You have the regular shoe that fits the clown's foot and then you have all that extra stuff, like big or bulging toes, leather stars, hearts, and zany colors."

His clown-cobbler days behind him, Zerobnick and his business partner, Jayne Woodward, now run what they believe may be the only shoe-making school in the world. Intensive workshops held in Port Townsend offer novice craftspeople, shoe designers, shoe company executives, and folks from around the world a chance to learn the ancient craft of shoemaking.

When he's not teaching others how to make shoes, Zerobnick is working on his dream of changing the footwear industry forever. He's created Digitoe, a computerized footwear system that might someday make it possible for everyone to have reasonably priced custom-made shoes that fit perfectly.

Even if your feet are bigger than Bozo's.

For more information about Zerobnick's clown clients and his shoe school, log on to www.shoeschool.com.

Steel Silhouettes
Raymond

Drive through the sleepy lumber town of Raymond on your way to Long Beach or South Bend and you'll notice that something is flat. Actually, you'll notice that 200 things are flat.

The 200 flat things are actually locally made steel sculptures that depict wild animals, people, and assorted man-made objects, and you'll see them scattered along the 3 miles of US 101 that pass through town.

At first it may be a bit unnerving to see a stationary elk or a bear on the side of the road. Or that pair of loggers who don't seem to be making much headway as they saw away on a rock with their whipsaw. But by then you've slowed down a bit and had time to spot the sculptures of deer, fishermen, kayakers, and Native Americans. And no doubt you're smiling and thinking to yourself, "Wow, Raymond must be a pretty cool place."

Which is exactly what town officials were hoping you'd be thinking when they decided back in 1993 to spend funds from a highway beautification grant on the Raymond Wildlife-Heritage Sculpture Corridor, or "that stretch of highway with all the metal cutouts."

If you pull over to check out what else Raymond has to offer, you'll discover the Northwest Carriage Museum, displaying horse-drawn vehicles dating from 1890 to 1910 at 314 Alder Street. At 310 Alder Street, the Willapa Seaport Museum displays all manner of logging memorabilia and marine artifacts. Nearby is the Dennis Company, an old-fashioned dry goods store at 146 Fifth Street that sports an 85-foot-long mural depicting loggers at work on a hillside above the Willapa River sometime in the early 1900s, when twenty lumber mills made this one of the more bustling logging communities in the Pacific Northwest. Back then, the town had a reputation as a pretty wild and wooly place. In an effort to dampen this image, city officials mounted a promotional campaign that touted Raymond as "The City That Does Things."

To see what they're doing in Raymond today, take I-5 to Chehalis, then head west on State Route 6. For more information about the steel sculptures, the museums, or the mural, contact the Raymond Chamber of Commerce at (360) 942-5419 or www.visit.willapabay.org.

Two hundred metal animals, loggers, fishermen, and kayakers wait along the roadside near Raymond.

WILLIE KIEL DIDN'T DIE HERE

Dr. William Kiel was the founder and spiritual leader of a Christian communal organization called the Bethelites. In 1855, having achieved financial success with communal farms and businesses in Bethel, Missouri, Kiel decided to lead a group over the Oregon Trail in order to establish a satellite branch of the group out west.

Kiel chose his nineteen-year-old son Willie to ride at the front of the thirty-five-unit wagon train heading west to Willapa Bay. Unfortunately, young Willie died from a bout of malaria just a few days before the trip was scheduled to begin. Determined to keep his promise to his son, William Kiel put Willie's body in a lead-lined coffin that was then filled with whiskey and sealed shut. The coffin rode out west with the wagon train, in the lead wagon, arriving along with the rest of the group in November 1855. William Kiel buried his son the day after Christmas.

William Kiel and the Bethelites stayed in Washington for just a short while. Within a year the group had moved south to Oregon, where they established the town of Aurora. Willie Kiel's grave is still here, though, about 3 miles east of Raymond on State Route 6.

We Stop for Elk

Sequim

In 1909 President Theodore Roosevelt established the 600,000-acre Mount Olympus National Monument, in part to protect a dwindling herd of elk now known as Roosevelt elk, or more formally, *Cervus elaphus roosevelti*. In 1938 Franklin D. Roosevelt signed into law an act creating Olympic National Park, which is now home to the largest population of the species.

A herd of about one hundred of these impressive beasts lives in and around the Dungeness Valley, making frequent forays across the highway near Sequim in search of tasty things to eat. As traffic in the area has increased, however, so has the number of unfortunate encounters between cars and elk on the highway.

After fences, dogs, and other methods of keeping jaywalking elk off the road were rejected, a biologist for the state of Washington hit upon

Roosevelt elk near Sequim wear electronic collars. Not to be fashionable, but to stay alive.

a novel idea: Attach radio transmitting collars to the elk so that their movement toward the highway triggers a warning sign for motorists.

These collars are the sort of modern-day forest accessory that scientists have been using to track the meanderings of wolves, bears, and other creatures. The twist here is that the signals coming from the collared elk in the herd set off a flashing warning light on a series of yellow and black ELK X-ING signs along US 101.

Though simple, the system seems to work. Curious drivers do indeed slow down when the elk signal is flashing, and very few of the animals have been killed since the program was put into place.

Don't Ditch This Celebration

Sequim

The state's oldest festival began as a celebration of a ditch.

In the summer of 1895, a group of Dungeness Valley settlers decided that if any real farming was going to get done in Sequim, they needed to figure out a way to get water from the Dungeness River uphill to their fields. Some Colorado transplants described the irrigation system they'd used successfully back east and suggested that it might work here.

Twenty or so hardy pioneers agreed to give it a try. After drawing up incorporation papers for a group they called the Prairie Ditch, they spent a winter digging a ditch and building the flume that would eventually make local irrigation a reality.

By spring the digging was done, and on May 1, 1896, folks came from miles around to witness the initial opening of the headgate. Although there was a momentary glitch in the system, the water soon flowed smoothly, and the success was feted with a gala picnic.

Sequim residents have celebrated that community irrigation project every year since, but now the Irrigation Festival is a weeklong party held in early May that includes a logging show, a truck and tractor pull, lawn mower races, a carnival, a strongman competition, flower and art shows, and a gala parade. For more information phone (360) 683-6197 or (800) 737-8462 or visit www.irrigationfestival.com.

John Wayne Marina
Sequim

About 2 miles east of the city of Sequim, on the west shore of scenic Sequim Bay, you'll find the John Wayne Marina, named for the late film star, who was a frequent visitor to this area. Wayne would bring his yacht, a converted minesweeper called the *Wild Goose,* into the bay during his many visits to the Puget Sound, and he purchased property in the area. In 1975 the Duke donated about twenty acres to the Port of Port Angeles, which developed the marina that now bears his name.

Even if you don't own a boat, you might want to stop by. The main marina building has two glass cases filled with John Wayne memorabilia, ranging from prop guns used in his movies to a shingle from the house he grew up in. There's also a bronze statue of the Duke, looking much as he did in the 1949 film *She Wore a Yellow Ribbon.*

Those who want to take home a souvenir of their visit to the actor's stomping grounds should stop in at Bosun's Locker, the marina gift shop, which conveniently carries a variety of John Wayne merchandise, including postcards, photographs, and life-size cardboard cutouts.

To get to the John Wayne Marina, follow US 101 north to the John Wayne Marina turnoff at Whitefeather Way. Turn right, then take a left at the stop sign to 2577 West Sequim Bay Road. Phone (360) 417-3440 or visit www.portofpd.com/marinas/john-wayne-marina.html.

Track Down a Good Night's Sleep
Sequim

Train fans and folks who seek out unusual spots where travelers can rest their weary heads have been making tracks to Sequim, where a series of cast-off cabooses have been transformed into a collection of cozy cottages-on-wheels. Operated by Olaf and Charlotte Protze, who say they happily traded careers in San Francisco for a life "playing with a life-size set of trains," the Red Caboose Getaway has a restored 85-foot-long steel 1937 Zephyr private dining car and a series of themed cabooses, each on its own track.

Conductors at the Red Caboose Gateway.

The *Casey Jones* caboose on track 1, for example, is a train enthusiast's dream-come-true, complete with an original conductor's desk and chair and the cupola intercom that was used to call the engineer with news of trouble with the load. On track 2, the *Orient Express* caboose has surprising touches, such as a two-person spa tub, a gas fireplace, and other upscale amenities. The Big Top–themed *Circus Caboose* on track 3 has a bathtub shaped like a Tunnel of Love boat, and the Western-themed caboose on track 4 has an antique claw-foot tub, pressed tin ceiling, and a video library stocked with Westerns.

Olaf Protze says the oldest caboose here dates from 1948, while the newest is from 1980, but all are real and part of a collection that just keeps on growing. He has ten tracks to fill, and at press time he was putting finishing touches on a lavender-themed caboose for track 5 and getting ready to get going on a caboose that will honor Paul Bunyan and another that will have a casino theme.

The Red Caboose Getaway is in Sequim, about two hours west of Seattle, on the corner of Old Coyote Way and West Sequim Bay Road at 24 Old Coyote Way. For more information call (360) 683-7350 or visit www.redcaboosegetaway.com

Aw, Shucks
Shelton

Oysters are big business in the southern Puget Sound region, and each year, on the first weekend in October, folks gather in Shelton to celebrate, shuck, and drink toasts to the bumpy bivalve.

Although OysterFest includes wine and beer tasting, oyster cook-offs, all sorts of dancing and eating, and an art and photography competition, the main attraction here is the oyster shucking contest, which is so fast paced that it might be over before you can even utter the festival's official name: the West Coast Oyster Shucking Championship and Washington State Seafood Festival.

There are actually two separate oyster shucking contests. On Saturday it's speed shucking, the object of which is to pry open two dozen oysters as quickly as possible. Many contestants in this category shuck oysters for a living at area oyster production houses and can finish the task in less than two minutes. Some can finish quicker: Hector Moreno did it in 1994 in 1 minute, 19 seconds. The slowest time on record was set in 1992, when Andy Conklin took just over 9 minutes, 34 seconds to finish the task.

On Sunday the half-shell competition is all about neatness and presentation. After contestants open two dozen oysters as quickly as they can, they must present them on a plate in the manner that they'd be served to a guest in a restaurant. So in this competition, judges add seconds to a contestant's time if there are errant pieces of shells on the plate or cuts in the oyster meat. While most contestants complete this task with a total score that hovers around two minutes, Pat Simon holds the record for slowest time at almost eleven minutes.

Want to try your hand at shucking or just eating oysters? The Oyster-Fest is held each year on the first full weekend in October at the Mason County Fairground on Sanderson Field. That's about a half mile north of Shelton, which is west of US 101. For more information call (800) 576-2021 or check out www.oysterfest.com.

Contestants in the oyster shucking contest are graded on speed and neatness.

NORTH AND NORTHWEST

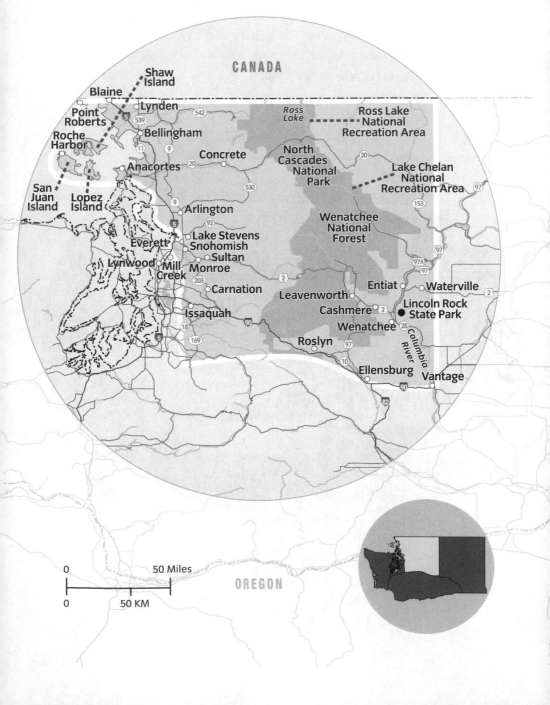

NORTH AND NORTHWEST

A big swatch of the state is included in this chapter. The area covered here starts in the San Juan Islands, heads east along Washington's northern border, and then dips down into the north central portion of the state.

The region includes Wenatchee and Ellensburg, two cities that have, at one time or another, each laid claim to being the state's center point. Why, we wondered, would they spend time fussing over points on the map when there are plenty of more unusual and alluring claims to fame? For example, Wenatchee holds the world's record for baking the largest apple pie, and Ellensburg is the home to a family of chimpanzees that communicates using sign language.

There are plenty of other natural and man-made wonders in this region, including a petrified forest, a meteor that once landed in court, and one of our favorites, a shrine to Possum Sweetheart, the hardest-working milk cow in Dairyville.

Woody Wonder
Arlington

A giant stump in Arlington has been a northwest curiosity for years. In the early 1900s it amused folks who traveled along State Route 99 near Marysville, but it's been moved several times since then. It now inspires awe and amusement at a rest stop on Interstate 5.

To see the stump, head north on I-5 and take exit 207, which is just north of Marysville.

Giant Northwest trees left behind giant stumps.

Spots for Shots
Snohomish County

These days, it seems as if there's a corporate coffeehouse on most every corner. In Snohomish County though, coffee cravers can line up for lattes at some truly unusual jaunty java joints. Here are a few spots where the shots of espresso are laced with a dose of whimsy.

In Arlington Cabooso Expresso (2730 172nd NE; 360-652-9835) is shaped just like, you guessed it, a red caboose, while HotSpot Coffee dispenses high-octane drinks from a shiny stand shaped like an oversize 1950s stove-top percolator sitting on a neon burner. You'll find it just off

I-5 at exit 208 (425-931-2272; www.hothothot coolcoolcool.com).

In Everett High Flying Espresso, near Paine Field Airport, helps customers get "buzzed" at a white and light-blue drive-thru topped by a giant coffee cup (2210 112th Street SW, 425-290-9069), while in Snohomish the folks at Maltby Cup O'Brew deliver jolts of caffeine from a bright-red stand shaped like a giant to-go cup complete with a straw (8731 Maltby Road; 425-760-0094).

Coffee to go!

Freshly-brewed coffee here!

Floundering around for a cup of coffee in Lynwood? The Mocha Boat (17412 Highway 99; 425-787-2628) is shaped like a yellow fishing boat on a sea of concrete, while over in Sultan they keep things turning at Windmill Espresso (933 Stevens Avenue; 360-799-0674).

Drinks for Everyone!
Anacortes

Anacortes resident Carrie M. White was a temperance activist who served a stint as the president of the Washington Women's Christian Temperance Union (WCTU). After White died in 1904, WCTU officials gave Anacortes a special drinking fountain in her honor.

Hailed by the local newspaper as "a convenience and luxury long needed," the decorative 9-foot-tall, 1,000-pound cast-iron and zinc fountain had three bowls of various sizes set at three different heights so that dogs, horses, and people could all gather round.

Because the fountain represented the WCTU's mission of advocating water instead of liquor, its installation in front of a downtown department store was not universally celebrated. In 1934, when it came time to widen the downtown streets, the fountain was moved to a local park, where it sat for more than forty years, sinking into a sad state of disrepair. Restoration efforts that began in 1974 have brought the fountain back to its bubbling glory, and it now graces the east lawn of the Anacortes History Museum.

So once again, there are no excuses for man, woman, or beast to go thirsty in Anacortes.

The WCTU Drinking Fountain is on the grounds of the Anacortes History Museum at 1305 Eighth Street in Anacortes. For more information phone (360) 293-1915 or visit http://museum.cityofanacortes.org/.

Built to honor a local temperance activist, this fountain served cold water to people, dogs, and horses.

Ways of the Wireless
Bellingham

Jonathan Winter is one of those guys who grew up listening to radio and tinkering with the tubes and wires that made the "magic boxes" sing. All manner of electric-powered objects found their way into his closets, and he eventually amassed several thousand radio tubes, speakers, microphones, early radios and television sets, Edison cylinders, 78 rpm records, and recordings of early radio programs. Finally, he decided to put all this stuff in a museum and invite folks to stop by to see—and hear—how it all worked.

While Winter's wired things were whirring away in Bellingham, John Jenkins was developing his own extensive collection of radios and objects related to the development of electricity. Having filled his attic and a specially built room in his house with objects dating from the 1600s up to the 1960s, he was quickly running out of space.

Luckily, the two collectors met up and realized that if they put their collections together they'd have one of the country's most extensive collections of radios and electronic devices. And if they put all these objects in a museum, they'd have the country's best museum devoted to electricity and radio. So that's what they did.

Of course, their American Museum of Radio and Electricity includes radios, televisions, and recording devices from the first half of the twentieth century, but it also features a good many very early, curious objects. Here you'll find some of Ben Franklin's static-electricity apparatus, Zamboni perpetual motion machines, a Parisian portable record player with a wind-up needle directly connected to a paper-cone speaker, an early fraudulent wireless telephone, and a full-size mock-up of the Marconi wireless room on the *Titanic*. Although Marconi's wireless was used to radio a distress call from the doomed ship to a nearby liner, the one radio operator on the other ship was asleep and missed the call. After that, ships were required to have someone monitoring the wireless twenty-four hours a day.

You can visit the American Museum of Radio and Electricity at 1312 Bay Street in downtown Bellingham. For information about hours and events, call (360) 738-3886 or log on to www.americanradiomuseum.org.

DID YOU KNOW?

Whatcom County boasts:

- Fourteen golf courses, more golf courses per capita than any other Pacific Northwest County. (*Golf Digest*)

- More than fifty espresso stands, the most drive-up espresso stands per capita in the state.

- Mount Baker, where a world record was set for the most snowfall in one year. In 1999, 1,140 inches of snow was recorded, topping the previous world record of 1,122 inches at Mount Rainier in 1971–1972. (National Climatic Data Center, August 1999)

BLACK CATS

If you're one of those superstitious people who think it's bad luck if a black cat crosses your path, be forewarned that Fairhaven, a historic six-square-block area of Bellingham, is a mecca for these midnight-colored meowers.

Why so many black cats? Locals trace the tale of the cats back to the late 1880s, when entrepreneur James Wardner established the Consolidated Black Cat Company on nearby Eliza Island in Bellingham Bay. Legend has it that, in a foreshadowing of Cruella De Vil, Wardner hatched a plan to breed black cats and then sell the pretty kitty pelts for $2 a piece to be used in furs. Some folks insist that this story is a hoax, but when you see all the black cats roaming the streets of the Fairhaven neighborhood, you can't help but wonder.

Whether or not felines in Fairhaven are descendants of lucky escapees from Wardner's kitty ranch, volunteers from the Fairhaven Kitty Committee help make sure these strays are well taken care of. They build kitty condos, operate a kitty adoption program, and provide cat food and medicine.

While black cats may roam the streets, the Fairhaven district has a more colorful past. Hoping to establish "the next Chicago," developers rushed to Fairhaven in the late 1880s to build hotels, taverns, an opera house, a concert garden, restaurants, and brothels. Today the brothels are gone, but the district bustles with restaurants, pubs, art galleries, antiques shops, bookstores, boutique hotels, and a spa. And those black cats. You can learn more about the history of Fairhaven from markers embedded in the sidewalks and from brass plaques mounted on many buildings. For more information call (360) 734-1790 or check out www.historicfairhaven.com.

Ski to Sea Race

Bellingham

For nearly thirty years Memorial Day weekend has signaled one big thing in Bellingham: the Ski to Sea Race. This 85-mile multistage relay race from Mount Baker to Bellingham is one of the most extreme examples of this sport you're likely to encounter. Race segments include downhill and cross-country skiing, running, bicycling, canoeing, mountain biking, and, finally, kayaking across Bellingham Bay to the Fairhaven neighborhood. Luckily, it's a team sport.

Racers with energy to spare—and folks who'd rather relax than push themselves to their outer physical limits—can choose instead to participate in the Ski to Sea Parade, the Ski to Sea Carnival, and the It All Ends in Fairhaven Street Festival.

The race has its roots in the Mount Baker Marathon, which was held from 1911 to 1913. That marathon, a foot race in which contestants had to run to the top of the mountain and back, was created by the conservation-minded Mount Baker Club, which was hoping to draw national attention to the beauty of the region. Unfortunately, the club had to discontinue the event when summer storms created hazardous trail conditions. One unlucky contestant fell into a crevasse, barely surviving his six-hour wait for rescue.

Revived as a safer but no less grueling relay race in 1973, the marathon now draws rugged participants from all over the world. To find out how you can participate as a contestant or a spectator, call (360) 734-1330 or check out www.skitosea.org.

Arching Peacefully
Blaine

Most people cross the border between Washington and Canada at the town of Blaine, a lovely spot on the interstate where traffic often backs up for miles as cars inch their way through customs. Rather than wait in line, many folks take the opportunity to wander through the forty-acre Peace Arch Park and ponder the Peace Arch, a huge symbol of friendly relations between Canada and the United States that straddles the boundary between Blaine, Washington, and Douglas, British Columbia.

The park has lovely grounds, plenty of flowers, intriguing sculptures, and a fun playground, but the big attraction is that huge white reinforced concrete arch, inscribed with CHILDREN OF A COMMON MOTHER on one side and BRETHREN DWELLING TOGETHER IN UNITY on the other.

Built between 1914 and 1921 at the urging of Washington State businessman, road builder, and philanthropist Sam Hill, the arch is one of the first structures built with earthquake resistance in mind. One of the only buildings listed on the Historic Registers of two countries, it also once contained timbers from two notable ships.

In 1921 Sam Hill, a Quaker, visited the Quakers in Jordans Village, England, who had used wood salvaged from the *Mayflower* to make a much-needed barn. They gave Hill a steel chest containing pieces of oak timber from the barn. When the Peace Arch was officially dedicated, Hill placed a piece of that timber inside, along with a piece of timber from the *Beaver,* a Hudson's Bay Company steamer ship that was the first to navigate the Pacific Ocean.

The wood mementos remained inside the arch until 1989, when it was discovered that they were experiencing water rot and weather damage. While the *Beaver* relic is now at Vancouver Maritime Museum, the timber from the *Mayflower* is still in storage, awaiting a drier and equally suitable home. (If you really want to see timber from the

Mayflower, there are a few pieces on display in that original steel chest at the Maryhill Museum near Goldendale in southern Washington.)

The Peace Arch is on I-5 at the United States–Canada border. For more information call (360) 332-8221 or check out www.peacearch park.org.

The Peace Arch straddles the border and is listed on the Historic Registers of both Canada and the United States.

Got Milk?

Carnation

World records are made to be broken, so in 1920 Segis Pietertje Prospect, a Holstein cow, and her favorite milker set out to break the record for annual milk production.

It wasn't so hard to do. Born at the Carnation Milk Farms in Carnation in 1913, Segis Pietertje Prospect, more commonly known as Possum Sweetheart, was already delivering above-average quantities of milk by the time Carl Glockerell was hired in 1919. He noticed that Possum Sweetheart seemed to produce at least twice as much milk as most other cows, and even more than any test cow at the farm.

Possum Sweetheart's reputation spread, and on December 19, 1919, Glockerell began a carefully monitored yearlong study to see just how

This moo-ving statue honors Possum Sweetheart. The well-loved Holstein set world records for milk production.

much milk she could deliver. One year later it was announced to great fanfare that the cow had produced just over 37,381 pounds of milk. Officials declared the feat udderly amazing: Possum Sweetheart had beat the previous world record by 3,956.4 pounds.

As befits a record-breaker, Possum Sweetheart got lots of attention, including a visit from then heavyweight boxing champion Jack Dempsey. Dempsey milked the appearance by taking off his coat, rolling up his sleeves, and setting up a pail under the much-heralded Holstein.

Sadly, Possum Sweetheart died in 1925. Three years later she was memorialized with a bronze plaque and a larger-than-life-size statue placed atop a 7-foot-high pedestal near the entrance to Carnation Farms.

Public tours of Carnation Farms (now owned by Nestlé), which included a visit to the milking parlor and the maternity barn, have been discontinued, with no official word on if or when they might be reinstated. However, it's possible to see the statue of Possum Sweetheart from the road.

Carnation is about 30 miles east of Seattle on State Route 203. The Farms are at 28901 NE Carnation Farm Road. For directions and more information call (425) 788-1511.

Confection of the Fairies

Cashmere

Folks traveling toward the Bavarian-themed town of Leavenworth usually make a point of stopping in Cashmere for something sweet. That's because for the past seventy-five years, Cashmere has been the factory headquarters for a popular candy that was originally created to make use of surplus fruits from an area orchard.

The candies were developed by Armen Tertsagian and Mark Balaban, two Armenian immigrants who bought an orchard near Cashmere. After discovering that they couldn't sell all that fresh fruit, they tried selling dehydrated apples and a jam called Applum that blended apples and plums, but they didn't realize success until they went back to their roots.

The business partners decided to try making rahat locoum, a Middle Eastern candy they remembered from childhood that mixed apples and walnuts with a coating of powdered sugar and cornstarch. Marketed initially in the Pacific Northwest as the "Confection of Fairies," the immediately popular and all-natural Aplets candies were soon followed by an apricot-and-walnut sweet known as Cotlets. The candies gained national attention when they were featured at the 1962 World's Fair in Seattle.

Today Aplets and Cotlets are still made in the Liberty Orchards Candy Kitchens, where a fifteen-minute factory tour ends with a variety of free samples. Liberty Orchards is located in Cashmere, about 6 miles off U.S. Highway 2, at 117 Mission Street on the corner of Aplets Way. For more information call (509) 782-4088 or log on to www.liberty orchards.com.

On Solid Ground

Concrete

The riverside town of Minnehaha was settled in 1871, but when it came time to put up a post office and plat out the streets, the simpler name of Baker was adopted.

Then the early 1900s version of big business and politics took over. The Superior Portland Cement Company built a plant in town on the west bank of the Baker River, and a competitor, the Washington Portland Cement Company, set up shop on the east bank of the river, spawning a new town that came to be known as "Cement City." The two towns merged in 1909 and, no doubt to curry favor and keep both business owners happy, townspeople agreed to adopt the new name of Concrete.

Although cement was the town's main industry, in the early days most Concrete buildings were made of wood. That is, until 1921, when fire swept through town, leaving only a church, the town hall, the library, and a few other buildings intact. When it came time to rebuild, the readily available and nonflammable concrete was the construction product of choice. To see what they did with all that cement, walk around town and read the plaques on the storefronts, or drive across the Henry Thompson Bridge, which was at one time the longest single-span reinforced concrete bridge in the world, and is now listed on the National Register of Historic Places.

To learn even more about Concrete's love affair with cement, and about the area's rich logging history, stop by the Concrete Heritage Museum at 7380 Thompson Avenue, one block off Main Street. The Concrete Chamber of Commerce hands out walking-tour brochures of the community at local businesses and campgrounds, and at the Concrete Saturday Market, which is held at the Concrete Senior Center building from May through Labor Day. Phone (360) 853-7042 or log on to www.concrete-wa.com.

THE SKY IS FALLING

In the early days of Concrete's cement production, the mile-long tramway that carried limestone from the quarry to the plant traveled right over Main Street. Before a safety net was installed, chunks of limestone would sometimes fall out of the buckets onto unsuspecting pedestrians below.

Talk to the Animals

Ellensburg

Perhaps you're old enough to remember when chimpanzees, our closest animal relatives, were sent into space to see if humans could survive a similar trip. Just imagine the stories those first space chimps could have told us if we'd had some way to communicate with them. Maybe the chimps could have spoken up about whether they were even interested in being shot out into space in the first place.

Well, the folks at the Chimpanzee and Human Communication Institute at Central Washington University in Ellensburg have been working on solving the chimp/human communication problem since 1966. Operating as a training center for students and a research center for scientists, the institute is home to Washoe, Loulis, Dar, and Tatu, four chimpanzees who have been taught American Sign Language. In addition to gesturing and vocalizing the same way chimps do in the wild, these primates also use sign language to communicate with humans and with each other.

Over the years, researchers at the institute have gotten to know Washoe, Loulis, Dar, and Tatu very well, and each chimp now has an extensive and informative biography. Washoe, it seems, loves looking at catalogs (especially shoe catalogs) and books. Loulis, who learned his first fifty-five signs from Washoe and the other chimps, loves watching human visitors, especially children. Fascinated by tools and mechanical devices, Dar likes to take things apart. Tatu, who is interested in how meals get prepared, signs most often about food. Another chimp, Moja, who died in June 2002, adored Velcro and liked dressing up in clothes.

You talkin' to me? Could be. Washoe is one of the chimps who learned American Sign Language.

Sound like a family you'd like to meet? Well, the center isn't generally open to the public, but you can sign up for a one-hour educational "Chimposium" in which you and your family can learn about chimpanzee culture and then get to see Washoe and his adopted family in action. After attending the one-hour session, you can come back for a more intensive four-and-a-half-hour Advanced Chimposium, which offers more detailed presentations and a closed-circuit dinner with the chimps.

The one-hour Chimposiums are offered Saturday and Sunday from March through November. Advanced Chimposiums are offered less often. To make a reservation, get directions, and find out about registration fees, call (509) 963-2244 or check out www.cwu.edu/~cwuchci.

Yard Full o' Fun
Ellensburg

Dick Elliot and his wife, Jane Orleman, are artists who surround themselves with art. Their creations, and those of their friends, spill out of their home, onto their home, into the front and back yards, and onto the fences.

What a delight! The couple's home has been declared an official folk art installation and has become a tourist attraction.

At Dick and Jane's Spot, as the corner of First and Pearl in downtown Ellensburg is called, you can stand on the sidewalk, peek into the yard, and spy a vast array of whimsical artwork made from all manner of odds and ends. Look over here and you'll see shiny reflectors and telephone-wire insulators. Over there you'll find the fence studded with bottle caps, spooky doll heads, and bent bicycle parts. Hanging on the second floor of the house is a giant fortune-teller's hand. And just about everywhere else there are kinetic sculptures, kooky mannequins, and just plain cool creations by dozens of other Northwest artists with a similarly bent sense of fun.

The curious can find out more about the art and the artists by reading the notes in the colorful kiosk at the side of the house. A guest book is there as well, so you can let the artistic duo know just how much fun they've added to your day.

Dick and Jane's Spot is located at 101 North Pearl Street in downtown Ellensburg, across from the police station. For more information see www.reflectorart.com.

Just about every inch of this Ellensburg yard is filled with whimsical folk art, making Dick and Jane's Spot a truly curious stop for the truly curious.

NO BULL

You'll find Richard S. Beyer's smile-inducing sculpture *Ellensburg Bull* sitting upright on a bench in Rotary Pavilion on Pearl Street in downtown Ellensburg. Passersby simply can't help smiling when they encounter this animal. Perhaps it's because he's got a jaunty pose and an outstretched arm that seems to invite you to snuggle in beside him. Or perhaps it's because the bull has a hat strategically placed over his lap.

If you enjoy the bull, look around for Beyer's *Kitt Coyote* in front of the Ellensburg Library at Third Avenue and Ruby Street. As inviting as the bull, this animal has more than a hat to keep him warm. Beyer has dressed the 7-foot coyote in a jacket, tie, pants, and shoes, and has given him a book to read.

Stone-Faced Lincoln

Entiat

Lincoln Rock State Park is an eighty-acre camping park on the east side of Lake Entiat, which was created when Rocky Reach Dam blocked the flow of the Columbia River north of Wenatchee. Not only is the park a popular place for swimming and waterskiing, there's a rock here that's a roadside attraction.

According to early newspaper accounts, back in 1889 Billy Schaft and Ed Ferguson took a picture of an unusual-looking outcropping of basalt rock high up on a hill. They claimed it looked just like Abraham Lincoln—if you stood in the right place—so the pair entered the picture in a photo contest being sponsored by the *Ladies' Home Journal.* To their surprise and delight, the photo won first prize and was published in the magazine. After that, the now nationally famous rock became officially known as Lincoln Rock. The area became a state park in 1980, when the state acquired the land.

Lincoln Rock State Park is located 7 miles north of East Wenatchee, on the eastern bank of the Columbia River. From East Wenatchee, drive north on State Route 2 for about 7 miles and look for the park signs. For more information phone (360) 902-8608 or check out www.parks.wa.gov/parks.

Look for Lincoln.

SOME SNOHOMISH COUNTY FACTOIDS

In addition to being the home of the world's largest building (the Boeing Company's assembly plant in Everett), Snohomish County boasts of having:

- more horses per capita than any other county in the United States

- ten ostrich farms

- the tallest American chestnut tree (106 feet tall and 20 feet in girth)

- lots of laundry (more than 5,500 pounds of laundry are washed each day aboard the USS *Abraham Lincoln*, the nuclear-powered aircraft carrier homeported in Everett)

- a "forgotten volcano," Glacier Peak

Bare Buns Fun Run

Issaquah

Washington State has many unusual parks, but certainly one of the most unusual is the Fraternity Snoqualmie Nudist Park. Incorporated as a nonprofit organization, this clothing-optional park, in operation since the 1930s, is the oldest and largest nudist park in the Northwest.

Forestia, as the park is called, covers forty forested acres and has all the amenities any great park might offer: a solar-heated swimming pool, a wading pool, spas, saunas, playgrounds, hiking trails, a clubhouse, and a gift shop. The only difference between this park and others is that folks choose whether to participate in the activities clothed or au naturel. It's a lifestyle thing.

The Fraternity Snoqualmie also sponsors the clothing-optional 5K "Bare Buns Fun Run West" each July on Tiger Mountain. Runners and walkers are invited to "Be Brave, Be Tough, Beat the Mountain in the Buff." There are strict rules of conduct, and no still or video cameras are allowed. (The Kaniksu Ranch, near Spokane in eastern Washington, holds what it calls the *original* Bare Buns Fun Run East, also in July.)

If you can't make it to either of the Bare Buns Fun Runs, don't fret. The group holds several other clothing-optional public events, including a music festival in August, called Nudestock.

Forestia is located on Tiger Mountain, just a few miles south of Issaquah, about a half-hour drive east of Seattle. For more information call (425) 392-NUDE or visit www.parkforestia.org.

Is It There or Isn't It?

Lake Stevens

Lake Stevens, just east of Everett, is named after the largest lake in Snohomish County. The historic downtown area, at the north end of the lake, is built on the former Rucker Mill site. According to legend, a locomotive that was used to move logs at the mill sank to the bottom of the lake, but divers never found anything. For years it was not unusual to walk into a local cafe or tavern and hear old-timers debating the point.

Finally, curiosity got the best of one local history buff, who somehow convinced the Navy SEALs to search the bottom of the cove as a training exercise. Within minutes they'd spotted the locomotive, buried and well preserved under about 20 feet of muck. They even produced a sonar picture of the sunken treasure to prove it.

You'd think that picture would have put the local debates to rest, but it didn't. Anne Whitsell from the Lake Stevens Historical Society says there are two old-timers, now in their nineties, who still refuse to believe that the mill would have let the locomotive fall off the track and into the water in the first place.

While those guys continue to argue, efforts are under way in Lake Stevens to get the necessary permits to raise the locomotive, restore it, and put it back on land in a local park. Maybe that will convince them.

To learn more about the Lake Stevens locomotive and the mill, stop by the Lake Stevens Historical Museum at 1802 124th Street in Lake Stevens; call (425) 334-3944 or log on to www.lakestevens.org.

Outdoor Oompahs
Leavenworth

Maybe instead of saying WILLKOMMEN IN LEAVENWORTH, the sign at the edge of town should say WARNING: YOU'RE STILL IN TIMBER COUNTRY, BUT IT SURE DOESN'T LOOK LIKE IT.

At one time Leavenworth was a healthy logging town with a profitable sawmill. But in the 1920s, after the Great Northern Railway rerouted around the town, the sawmill closed down. For years the town was in danger of disappearing completely.

In the early 1960s town officials struck on the idea of turning the town into a tourist destination. Taking a cue from the lovely alpine hills that surround the area, the folks in Leavenworth all agreed to transform the town into a faux Bavarian village. Architectural standards were drawn up to help downtown business owners remodel their storefronts. Speakers were installed to pipe theme music onto the streets. Shops started stocking German-made crafts and souvenirs. Restaurants began serving German food, bars poured German beer and wine, and oompah bands performed regularly in the town square.

Corny as it all sounds, it worked! Today Leavenworth draws more than a million tourists a year. To be sure, they're drawn by the quaintness and quirkiness of the town, but they're also lured here by the numerous festivals held throughout the year. Highlights include the Autumn Leaf Festival, a Christmas Lighting Ceremony, a Bavarian Icefest, a German Mardi Gras, and, of course, an Octoberfest.

Leavenworth is located at the foot of the Cascade Mountain Range, on US 2. For more information call the Leavenworth Chamber of Commerce at (509) 548-5807 or check the chamber's Web site, www.leavenworth.org.

Between the Covers
Leavenworth

Not everyplace in Leavenworth is a mandatory trip to Bavaria. For a change of pace, the folks at the local bookstore have set up a themed inn over their store that lets visitors journey to the places described by well-known authors.

At the Innsbrucker Inn, also known as the Inn of Six Authors, each room is decorated to evoke the work of a different author. The Anne Morrow Lindbergh suite is a wicker-filled room decorated to resemble Lindbergh's seaside cottage in the Yorkshire Dales. The Sherlock Holmes suite has the look of a Victorian study, while the room honoring humorist Patrick McManus is set up as a rustic, trophy-filled hunting lodge. The suite that pays homage to the author of *The Lion, the Witch, and the Wardrobe*, C. S. Lewis, is a family-size room that promises to take guests "on a walk through the wardrobe to the land of Narnia." Cutest of all, though, is the flowery room inspired by Frances Hodgson Burnett's *The Secret Garden*.

If you want to be sure a copy of the appropriate book is on your pillow so you can curl up and read as soon as you arrive, you can even place a book order when you make your reservation.

The Innsbrucker Inn is located at 703 US 2 in Leavenworth, right over A Book for All Seasons. For more information call (509) 548-1451 or go online and check the inn's Web site, www.innsbruckerinn.com.

Sometimes You Feel Like a Nut

Leavenworth

My skinny, blind grandfather could always amaze me and my brothers by cracking open two walnuts by squeezing them with one hand. When I grew up, I learned that most people used some sort of utensil to get this job done, and that over the centuries a great number of creative and beautiful devices have been created for just this purpose.

In fact, probably the best place to learn about how creative folks have gotten in their zeal to break open nuts is at the Nutcracker Museum, in the Bavarian-themed town of Leavenworth, where nutcrackers of every shape and size are lined up, ready to reveal the history of eating nuts.

Nutcracker Museum curator Arlene Wagner with one of her nut-loving friends.

The collection belongs to Arlene Wagner, a former ballet teacher who produced the famous *Nutcracker* ballet for many years. Much like the ballet's Clara, Arlene became entranced with wooden toy soldier nutcrackers and started a collection. As these things go, she got a bit carried away. Today, Arlene and her husband, George, show off their 5,000-plus nutcrackers at the museum above their store, which sells—you guessed it—nutcrackers.

The collection includes nutcrackers of every shape, size, and material. Pretty much every different style of wooden toy soldier nutcracker is here, as well as Asian betel cutters, figural crackers from Europe, and a wide variety of the nutty devices from around the world, made out of everything from ivory, brass, and porcelain to bone and silver. Of special interest are the tiny nutcracker nestled in a walnut shell and the walking sticks that have working nutcrackers on top. There are also delightful nutcrackers in the shape of dogs, squirrels, crocodiles, and eagles, and others depicting characters ranging from Darth Vader and Robin Hood to the Sugar Plum Fairy.

Some of the nutcrackers on display are very early, crudely crafted models, obviously designed simply to get the job done, but others were created as fine works of very expensive art (I suspect some of them were just for show). Put to use or not, the nutcrackers in the collection represent the different methods of cracking nuts: direct or indirect pressure, screw, or percussion. So, unless your grandfather can crack walnuts with his bare hands, you can choose what sort of nutcracker you'd use to crack the shells of your favorite nuts.

The Nutcracker Museum, a National Heritage Foundation, is located at 735 Front Street in downtown Leavenworth. It's open afternoons from May through October and on weekends from November through April. No squirrels allowed. For more information call (800) 892-3989 or visit www.nutcrackermuseum.com.

Town Hawk
Lopez Island

In general, red-tailed hawks are easy to spot. Brown with reddish tones, they're about twice the size of crows, with wingspans of about 3 feet. But for about twenty-five years, one unusual hawk living on the south end of Lopez Island was impossible to miss: a rare albino red-tailed bird with all-white feathers except for a few tail feathers that retained the typical red and brown tones.

According to the folks at the Lopez Island Historical Museum, it was unusual for the albino hawk to survive so long, but she did so perhaps because "she was a good hunter and a regular at many area chicken coops. We all knew her and we all looked out for her."

This albino hawk lived on Lopez Island.

As the bird aged, however, her eyesight began to fail. Sadly, one morning she was discovered dead after getting tangled up in the wire of one of the chicken coops she visited frequently. The couple who found her there gently untangled her from the wires, put her in their freezer, and called the historical museum. A local taxidermist prepared the bird for display.

Now each summer the couple who found the albino hawk in their chicken coop stop by the museum "to check on their girl" and to pay their respects. You can, too. The Lopez Island Historical Museum is open from May through September. In addition to that taxidermied albino red-tailed hawk, the museum also displays four owls and a Trumpeter swan, which also died after getting hung up on a fence wire. The museum is open afternoons, Wednesday through Sunday, from May through September. For directions and more information call (360) 468-2049 or visit www.rockisland.com/~lopezmuseum/.

Dutch Oasis
Lynden

Even though it's just 12 miles north of Bellingham and only 3 miles south of the Canadian border, visitors can't help but think they've stumbled into old-time Amsterdam when they arrive in the town of Lynden. That's because residents here are so darn proud of their Dutch ancestry that they've re-created a bit of old-time Holland right in the center of town.

Dutch Old Town, as they call it, has a 72-foot-tall working windmill that doubles as an inn, a 150-foot meandering indoor canal, and a Dutch-themed mall with a faux cobblestone street and shops that sell everything from Dutch lace to wooden shoes and Delftware. Restaurants are staffed by waiters and waitresses in native dress, and Dutch bakeries dot the streets.

Lynden is a sweet place to stop most anytime of the year, but for a real taste of the old country, try to show up for Holland Days on the first weekend in May. Festivities include draft horse rides, a parade, live music and "klompen dancing," and the traditional sweeping of the streets.

Even if you're not up for a Dutch treat, it's worth stopping in Lynden to visit the Lynden Pioneer Museum at 217 West Front Street (360-354-3675 or www.lyndenpioneermuseum .com). The town's turn-of-the-twentieth-century Main Street has been lovingly re-created inside the museum, and the basement is just chock-full of buggies, wagons, trucks, and antique cars.

Lynden is located north of Bellingham, on State Route 395. For more information call (360) 354-5995 or log on to www.lynde.org.

This giant windmill isn't in Holland. It's in downtown Lynden, home of the annual Holland Days celebration.

Behemoth Bun
Mill Creek

In an effort to make the 2004 grand opening of the House of Bread bakery in Mill Creek a truly grand affair, owners Wayne and Anita Warren and their crew whipped up a special treat: a 90-pound cinnamon roll that was then cut up and handed out for free. But Wayne Warren isn't one to rest on his buns. So when he read an article about a Kansas baker who'd made a supposedly unbeatable 150-pound cinnamon roll, Warren took up the challenge. He announced that he'd not only bust the Kansas baker's 150-pound cinnamon bun record, but he'd bake a bun big enough to earn a place in the *Guinness Book of World Records*.

And he did.

Well, actually the community of Mill Creek did. Under the watchful eyes of the mayor and local pastry lovers, the staff of the House of Bread shaped 180 pounds of dough into one gigantic cinnamon roll. Officers from the local police department helped load the raw roll into the oven and, two hours later, a team of local firemen helped haul the pastry out. Once the bun was cooled and covered with icing, officials from the Washington State Department of Agriculture stepped in. First a food safety officer declared that the bun was indeed an edible, albeit unusually large, cinnamon roll. Then a weights and measures inspector certified the weight of the bun at a hefty 246.5 pounds and its official size as 6 feet in diameter. Photographs and videotapes were made and, once all the paperwork was ready to be sent off to the *Guinness Book of World Records*, there was just one thing left to do: eat

World's Largest Cinnamon Bun.

the behemoth bun. Luckily, about 1,000 onlookers were on hand to help out.

Wayne Warren is happy to report that his 246.5-pound cinnamon roll is indeed now certified as the world's largest. But, as we mentioned above, Warren isn't one to rest on his buns. For a local festival that took place in Mill Creek in 2006, the folks at the House of Bread made an even bigger cinnamon roll. This one weighed in, unofficially, at 276 pounds. "We already hold the big bun record," says House of Bread owner Wayne Warren, "so we didn't go through all that extra trouble of getting to certify this creation. We just cut it up and let folks eat it."

The House of Bread is located in the new Mill Creek Town Center at 15224 Main Street. In addition to their "regular" everyday five-ounce cinnamon rolls, the bakery makes made-from-scratch breads six days a week. For directions and more information call (425) 385-8553 or visit www.houseofbreadwa.com.

Want to make your own record-breaking cinnamon roll?
Start with these ingredients:

13.7 cups honey

112.1 lbs. white flour

34.3 oz. yeast

34.3 oz. salt

60.3 lbs. water

40 lbs. brown sugar cinnamon

10 lbs. butter

40 lbs. icing

No raisins

Leapin' Lizards!!
Monroe

Most folks would shy away from a place filled with venomous snakes, giant hairy spiders, and cockroaches big as kittens, but because the Washington Serpentarium promises folks that most of these creatures stay locked up behind glass, it draws a crowd.

Scott Petersen—with friend.

Scott Petersen, who prefers to be known as the Reptile Man, is one of those people who was born with a fascination for reptiles. "When I started walking, I walked out of the house and started catching snakes and things," he says. "Perhaps I inherited the gene from my grandfather, who was a scientist who studied bugs." However he came to love these creatures, Petersen now has more than 200 creepy-crawlies you can visit at the Washington Serpentarium. Slither on in and you'll get to meet a black Pakistan cobra, a green mamba, and a puff adder. Press your face to the glass to examine a monkey tail skink, a bearded dragon, and a Brazilian pink tarantula. Don't forget to visit the albino alligator, the only one in the Pacific Northwest, or the two-headed turtle, a popular new attraction. Spend an afternoon here, and not only will you get to see one of the most comprehensive collections of reptiles on the West Coast, if you're brave enough, you'll even get a chance to handle some of the more friendly animals.

You can head up to Monroe to visit all the creatures at the Washington Serpentarium, or you can have the Reptile Man bring an assortment of animals to you. As you'd imagine, Petersen is a welcome guest at school assemblies, where kids clamor for a chance to pet the pythons or touch the tarantulas while learning about the importance of all animals in the balance of nature. When the Reptile Man is booked for corporate appearances with adults in attendance, the scene is surprisingly quite similar. Most everyone, it seems, is a sucker for serpents.

Just in case having tarantulas and giant snakes in your home, school, or office makes you nervous, rest assured that the Reptile Man is fully insured. The Washington Serpentarium is located 1 mile east of Monroe, at 22715-B on US 2. For more information call (360) 668-8204 or check out www.reptileman.com.

Which Side Are You On?

Point Roberts

You can drive a car, fly a small plane, motor your boat, walk, ride a bicycle, or even swim to Point Roberts, but whatever means you choose to get there, please remember to bring some form of identification. That's because although Point Roberts is technically in the United States, the only easy way to get there is to drive through a portion of Canada.

Technically part of Washington's Whatcom County, Point Roberts, a 5-mile tip of land, is a peninsula separated from the United States by water and British Columbia's mainland. Looking at it on a map, it seems as if Point Roberts should be part of Canada, but the land dips below the forty-ninth parallel, which is the official boundary between the United States and Canada.

A small marker in Monument Park, at the very end of Marine Drive, notes the longitude and latitude at the westernmost spot on the border between the United States and Canada. Here, nothing more than a ditch separates the two countries. Head south on Marine Drive, though, and you'll arrive at Lighthouse Park, where the views are a bit more enticing. The twenty-two acre park has a half-mile beach and a lookout platform that offers a great perch for watching sunsets and keeping an eye out for the resident pods of orca whales.

To Point Roberts: Go north on I-5 north to Peace Arch border crossing at Blaine. Once in Canada, take Highway 99 to Highway 17, then travel west for 5 miles to the Tsawwassen exit where 56th Street will bring you to Point Roberts—and back into Washington State. If you want to make your approach via United States territory, you'll need to arrive by water. For more information contact the Point Roberts Chamber of Commerce at (360) 945-2313 or visit the chamber's Web site at www.pointrobertschamber.com.

What's a Girl to Do?

Roslyn

In 1883 coal was discovered in the hills outside Roslyn; by 1901 more than one million tons of coal were being mined and shipped out of the area each year. Production declined after peaking in the 1920s, stopping completely in the 1960s, when the last coal mine shut down. In between, jobs in the mines provided modestly paying but honest work to thousands of men and at least one determined woman.

"Tony" Bailey worked as a loader for the Northwest Improvement Company in mine number 9 for eleven months beginning in July 1949. At that time state law prohibited girls and young women from getting jobs around the actual workings of a mine. Nineteen-year-old Gloria Bailey, just in from Montana, had a sick mother to support and a dream of opening a cafe. Because mine work paid better than any other job in town, Gloria decided to become "Tony" and go to work in the mines. Described by coworkers as a "darned good worker," Bailey's cover was blown when the chief of police spotted Tony going in and out of the women's restroom.

Bailey's story is only one of the colorful local stories revealed at the Roslyn Historical Museum, which displays an eclectic array of mining memorabilia as well as old household appliances, photographs, and some very unusual gadgets.

The Roslyn Historical Museum is in downtown Roslyn, at 203 Pennsylvania Avenue. It's near the Roslyn Cafe, a gathering spot seen in the television show *Northern Exposure,* which used pretty much the entire town and its residents as stand-ins for the Alaskan town of Cicely. For more information phone (509) 649–2776 or see www.cleelumroslyn.org/activities/museums.html.

TOMBSTONE TESTAMENTS

When coal mining in Roslyn was at its peak, the city boasted a population of more than 4,000 people from as many as twenty-six different ethnic groups. The community also had dozens of fraternal and ethnic organizations, which helped residents deal with all manner of issues, including marriages, health care, and death.

That's why the Roslyn Cemetery, covering fifteen acres of a hillside just west of town, is actually about twenty-six separate cemeteries. Discrete plots of land represent pretty much every ethnic, religious, civic, and veteran's organization that served the diverse population that flocked here to eke out a living doing dangerous work underground.

Founded in 1885, the Old City Cemetery is the oldest cemetery in town. It contains the remains of miners killed in coal-mining explosions, and one lone grave for an unknown person. There are also sections dedicated to Druids, Old Knights of Pythias, Serbians, foresters, and veterans.

You'll find many ornate headstones here, some so worn that you can barely make out the names engraved on them, and several mausoleums.

To tour the Roslyn Cemetery, head west on Pennsylvania Avenue from downtown Roslyn and follow the signs up the hill.

Roslyn's twenty-six cemeteries contain many unusual headstones and reflect the community's diverse ethnic heritage.

Log Float Lullabies

Ross Lake

Why check into a hotel with a waterbed (are there any of these left?) when you can get away from it all at an unusual lodge where your entire room floats on water?

That's what's offered at the remote Ross Lake Resort in the North Cascades National Park area. First, though, you have to get there, and that's an adventure all on its own.

Begin by driving to Diablo Dam on State Route 20. That's about three hours from Seattle. From there, catch a ride to the end of Diablo Lake on the *Seattle City Light* tugboat. Then it's a truck ride to Ross Lake. The reward? Once you're at the lake, you can check into one of the twelve cabins or three bunkhouses built on log pallets that float gently on the water. Be forewarned: This place is very remote, and although towels, bedding, tableware, and pots and pans are provided, you must remember to bring your own food as there are no restaurants or stores nearby.

Those who have made the trek to the lake and out to the resort swear that it's most definitely worth the trouble. Especially if you're looking for solitude and the chance to do some hiking, kayaking, or fishing in pristine surroundings on a lake that's 20 miles long, 1,600 feet deep, and up to 2 miles wide.

Ross Lake Resort is open mid-June to October. For reservations and information contact the resort at (206) 386-4437 or www.rosslake resort.com.

Poor Piggy
San Juan Island

In the mid-1800s some sheep, a pig, and a debate over the exact location of the international border on San Juan Island came close to sparking a full-scale war between England and the United States.

A treaty made in 1846 placed the boundary at the forty-ninth parallel to the west coast of the mainland and then to "the middle of the channel which separates the continent from Vancouver's Island." But which channel? England claimed Rosario Strait as the separating channel, which meant the San Juan Islands were theirs. The United States also claimed ownership of the San Juan Islands, based on the belief that Haro Strait was the channel referred to in the treaty.

Things started heating up in 1855, when the United States tried unsuccessfully to collect taxes from a sheep farm owned by the British Hudson's Bay Company on San Juan Island. In lieu of payment, local authorities confiscated several British rams and auctioned them off. A few years later, the dispute escalated to near-war conditions after an unrepentant American farmer shot a Hudson's Bay Company pig he discovered rooting around in his potato patch.

The feud prompted the construction of forts at English Camp and American Camp and joint military occupation of San Juan Island until 1872, when Kaiser Wilhelm I of Germany, acting as arbitrator, declared the United States the rightful owner of the island.

You can learn more about the whole long-drawn-out but ultimately peaceful event at the English Camp, 10 miles northwest of Friday Harbor, and the American Camp, on the southeastern tip of the island, about 6 miles from Friday Harbor. Both sites are part of the San Juan Island National Historic Park, which hosts a Pig War Festival each August at English Camp. The celebration includes re-creations of camp life, music, period crafts, blacksmithing, sewing, and carpentry.

For specific dates and more information, contact San Juan Island National Historic Park at (360) 378-2902 or www.nps.gov/sajh.

Supersized Greetings

San Juan Islands

Three pods of black and white orca whales (aka "killer whales"), known as the Southern Resident Community or the Salish Sea Orcas, live and play In the waters around the San Juan Islands. It's a treat whenever a human gets a glimpse of one or more of these impressive animals off-shore, but if you're truly lucky, you'll be on hand when all three pods are in town. Then you may get to witness a rarely observed eighty-five-whale "Greeting Ceremony."

Orcas lining up to say hello.

According to the Orca Network, a well-known conservation organization based on Whidbey Island, the three pods sometimes hold this ritualized greeting ceremony after they have been apart. During the ceremony each pod lines up abreast on the surface, and then the whales approach each other, one by one, until the lines dissolve. After that, the whales greet, rub together, and play in what seems like a truly festive celebration that sometimes lasts for days.

Want to party with the whales or find out more about *Orcinus orca*? The Whale Museum in Friday Harbor has whale skeletons, a whale phone booth where you can listen in on whale conversations, and a whale hotline for public sightings (800-562-8832). The museum is located at 62 First Street N in Friday Harbor. For hours and more information call (360) 378-4710 or visit www.whalemuseum.org. For more information about Orcas and the Greeting Ceremony, contact the Orca Network at www.orcanetwork.org.

Memorial to Lime
San Juan Island/Roche Harbor

Lime, made by heating limestone to extremely high temperatures, is an age-old chemical that has been used as an ingredient in everything from cement and steel to paper and plaster.

In 1886, shortly after a huge ledge of some of the world's purest limestone was discovered at Roche Harbor, John S. McMillan established the Tacoma and Roche Harbor Lime and Cement Company. Crushed limestone from a quarter-mile-long quarry was fed into a battery of brick-lined kilns, which created the necessary heat to turn the rock into 200-pound barrels of lime. By 1890 up to 1,500 barrels of lime were being produced each day, making this the largest lime works west of the Mississippi and making McMillan a very rich man.

You'll need to know the Masonic Order symbols—or take along the descriptive brochure—to fully appreciate the meaning of this unfinished family mosoleum.

John Wayne soaked here.

McMillan, who built a company town to go along with his limestone business, owned the hotel, a home overlooking the harbor, cottages and bunkhouses occupied by employees, a general store, barns, a church, and the schoolhouse. The quarries closed in 1946, but today you can hike around the grounds, visit the general store, and stay in the Hotel de Haro, which is now on the National Register of Historic Places. Theodore Roosevelt stayed here in 1906 and again in 1907; the room he stayed in (Room 2A) is now the Presidential Suite. Roosevelt also signed the guest book displayed in the lobby. Much later, actor John Wayne was a regular visitor. The claw-foot tub he enjoyed soaking in is now in the women's bathroom on the hotel's second floor.

Tucked into the woods about a mile up the road from the hotel, you'll find the very strange McMillan family mausoleum. Full of Masonic Order symbolism, this stone temple has a limestone table at its center, surrounded by four stone chairs that contain the ashes of McMillan and his family members. The sets of three, five, and seven steps, the broken and unbroken columns, the pillars, and numerous other elements in the mausoleum all have special and very specific meanings, which are described in extreme detail in a brochure you can pick up at the Hotel de Haro. One thing not explained, however, is why McMillan's family set aside no funds to maintain the plants, flowers, and shrubs around the mausoleum or why the family never finished McMillan's design. The mausoleum was supposed to have a bronze dome with a Maltese cross on top.

Roche Harbor is located on the north tip of San Juan Island, which is accessible by Washington State Ferry from Anacortes. For more information phone (800) 451-8910 or (360) 378-2155 or log on to www .rocheharbor.com.

Blessed Ferry Riders
Shaw Island

From 1976 until 2004 anyone who took the ferry to tiny Shaw Island in the San Juan Islands was blessed. Literally. That's because an order of nuns, four Franciscan Sisters of the Eucharist, operated the ferry dock here, giving the Blessing of St. Francis to each boatload of ferry riders they sent off.

The nuns were a busy bunch. In addition to operating the ferry landing in long brown habits and bright safety vests, the nuns also operated the general store at the ferry landing (the island's one commercial business) and offered computer training, outdoor classes for children, counseling, and music instruction. But as the nuns reached their sixties and seventies, they decided it was time to retire. So they gave up the ferry contract, closed their businesses, sold their property, and moved to a Franciscan center in Oregon. These days the ferry landing is operated by a local couple who pass out warm, welcoming smiles instead of blessings.

The fact that there's just one store and few other amenities seems to suit the 200 or so residents of this 5,000-acre island just fine. That includes the order of cloistered Benedictine nuns who live at Our Lady of the Rock Monastery and Retreat tucked into forest and farmland in the center of the island. These nuns breed and care for llamas, alpacas, and several rare breeds of animals, including Kerry cattle, (Scottish) Highland cattle, and Cotswold sheep. They also raise poultry, grow flowers, vegetables, and herbs, and create award-winning wool blankets and other craft items. When these nuns aren't working, they're praying. They live according to the motto of the Order of Saint Benedict—*Ora et Labora* (to pray and to work)—celebrating Mass eight times a day and singing lovely Gregorian chants. To plan a visit call (360) 468-2321 or check out www.rockisland.com/~mhildegard/.

WHY STAY HOME?

Born and raised in New Zealand, Helen Thayer started climbing mountains when she was just nine. Perhaps she caught the bug from world-famous mountain climber Sir Edmund Hillary, who was a family friend. Or maybe she's just a natural-born adventurer.

As a young woman, Thayer competed in international track and field competitions, winning the U.S. Women's National Luge title when she was thirty-six years old. In 1988, at the age of fifty, Thayer became the first woman to solo any of the world's poles when she walked alone to the magnetic North Pole. To get there, she traveled 350 miles in twenty-seven days, pulling her own sled, food, and supplies. Her dog, Charlie, came along to ward off hungry polar bears.

Good thing she survived, because after conquering the North Pole, Thayer has just kept going. In 1996 she and her husband, Bill, walked across the Sahara Desert, following an ancient camel trade route for 2,400 miles. They have made other awe-inspiring trips together, like trekking through southern Alaska with a herd of 500,000 caribou and crossing the entire length of the Mongolian Gobi Desert.

Why does she do it? Thayer loves setting big goals and then exceeding them. She also loves writing about her adventures, inspiring others to reach higher than they ever expected, and planning her next big expedition.

You can read about Helen Thayer's visit to the North Pole and her other adventures at www.helen thayer.com.

Helen Thayer and her dog, Charlie, trekked to the magnetic North Pole. Why? Because it was there, silly.

Amazing Maize Maze
Snohomish

In 1984 Ben and Carol Krause bought a patch of land in Snohomish that had been operating as a farm since the early 1900s and as a dairy since the 1920s. They tried their hand at milking cows for a few years, but in 1997 decided to turn their acreage into The Farm, a destination spot for field trips and family entertainment. Where cows once roamed, there's now a putting course, a U-pick flower patch, some pigs, a few goats, cornfields, and, each fall, a great field of pumpkins. It's what the Krauses do to their cornfield each year, however, that warrants an entry here.

Each summer, when the sweet corn has ripened, the cornfield is transformed into a twelve-acre maze in the shape of the state of Washington. Wending through the maize are more than 250 carefully roped off "roads" that take the adventurous traveler from the Idaho border south to Pullman and west to Seattle or, if you're not too good at mazes, back and forth across the state. Along the way are signs that point out about 400 state landmarks, including the Space Needle, Grand Coulee Dam, and the Peace Arch. Maps of the maze, complete with road closures and shortcuts, are issued at the border; if you're game, you can even try making your way through the maize maze at night by moonlight or flashlight.

The Farm is located at 7301 Rivershore Road in Snohomish. For hours, fees, and more information, call (425) 334-9820 or check out www.thefarm1.com.

The Space Needle is just one of the landmarks that can help you make your way through the maize maze.

MORE MAZES

Over the past few years, corn mazes have become increasingly popular all over Snohomish County. In addition to The Farm's Washington State maze, there are about a half dozen other farms in the county where the owners spend their winter evenings dreaming up new themes for the corn mazes they'll carve in the fall. Pirate ships, *The Wizard of Oz,* nursery rhymes, farm facts, and geographic wonders of the world have all cropped up as themes. As Halloween approaches, several farms go all out with fun but fright-filled mazes.

For more information about Snohomish County corn mazes, including maps, themes, and directions, call (425) 644-4331 or check out www.snohomish.org and look for "Agricultural Tourism" under the "Things To Do" tab.

Running Away with the View

Vantage

Travelers and wild-horse fans making their way through central Washington on Interstate 90 are in for a treat. On a lonely mesa overlooking the Columbia River there's a huge sculpture of fifteen life-size metal horses that look as if they've been frozen midstampede. Funded by private donations and created by Chewelah sculptor David Govedare, this massive piece of outdoor art was presented as a gift during Washington's centennial celebration in 1989 and placed on state-owned land.

Govedare, who created the sculpture in remembrance of the days when thousands of wild horses roamed the surrounding countryside, hopes people viewing the 1,000-pound work will think of freedom and of the fragile balance that exists between humans, animals, and the environment. As massive and dramatic as the sculpture is, though, it's not quite

These fifteen life-size metal horses seem to race along a mesa overlooking Interstate 90. They just never get anywhere.

finished. Govedare's original plan for *Grandfather Cuts Loose the Ponies* included a thirteen-ton, 36-foot-diameter metal basket decorated with symbols of land, water, sky, and "the human spirit." He wanted the horses to appear to be running out of the tilted basket as a commemoration of the Great Spirit's gift of horses to this planet. Unfortunately, he ran out of funds and Govedare is still hoping to raise the $300,000 needed to complete the project.

In the meantime Govedare visits his artwork quite regularly. He'll pull over at a viewpoint along the highway on I-90 and join other travelers clicking away with their cameras, or hike up the hill to hang out with his horses and fix any damage the area's high winds and severe weather may have caused.

Grandfather Cuts Loose the Ponies is on a plateau on the north side of I-90, just east of Vantage. The best viewing spot is at Wanapum Vista, on eastbound I-90, 3 miles east of Vantage.

Don't Kick the Rocks

Vantage

Smack-dab in the center of Washington State there's a most unusual forest overlooking the Columbia River. Like all forests, it's got trees, but with 7,500 acres of fossilized trees, this is the largest stone forest in the world.

How did it get here? Well, it seems that fifteen to twenty million years ago, when this area was mostly lakes and swamps, logs and limbs fell into the lakes and were buried and sealed by lava that welled up through cracks in the earth's surface. The lava halted the wood's natural decomposition, and minerals from the lava eventually replaced the wood's cell structure, creating perfectly preserved fossilized "trees of stone." Later, much later, Ice Age floods, natural erosion, wind, rain, and excavation efforts by humans removed enough covering material to reveal the petrified trees.

So what you'll see today on the lovely ¾-mile hike along the Trees of Stone Interpretive Trail are examples of some of the more than 200 species of fossilized trees that have been discovered here, including Douglas fir, spruce, elm, and the ginkgo, the rarest form of fossilized wood.

Be sure to stop at the Ginkgo Petrified Forest Interpretive Center, which exhibits "raw" petrified samples that look exactly like sections of living trees, and about 200 slices of lovely polished petrified wood. Most curious, though, is the "picture wood" display, slices of fossilized wood that contain Mother Nature's drawings of lovely landscapes and images that look exactly like portraits of a young girl, some ducks floating on a pond, Jimmy Durante, a baboon, and Dagwood Bumstead.

The Ginkgo Petrified Forest and Interpretive Center is located in Vantage, where I-90 crosses the Columbia River. For hours and more information call (509) 856-2700 or visit www.parks.wa.gov and search under "Park Information."

It Ain't Heavy, It's Our Meteorite

Waterville

In 1917 a major meteor shower filled the skies over central Washington. In the following years folks in and around the Waterville area stumbled across three large nickel-iron meteorites that together weighed in at more than 112 pounds.

One of these specimens was found by farmer Fred Fachnie when it got caught in his combine during harvest season. The 82½-pound marvel, later known as the Waterville Meteorite, found its way into both the meteor history records and the courts.

In 1925 Fachnie loaned his meteorite to a museum in Tacoma, which sliced off almost ten pounds of the space rock and then tried to claim ownership of it. Legal battles ensued, but in 1963 the meteorite was returned home to Waterville, a shy bit lighter but much more famous than when it left. It now resides in the Douglas County Historical Museum, alongside a wonderful collection of rocks and minerals, some of which glow in the dark.

In addition to rocks and meteorites, the museum exhibits a few other unusual items. Most notable among them is a model of a cathedral, complete with pipe organ, choir loft bells, and six tiny pews all made out of 3,500 Popsicle sticks. There's also a great collection of barbed wire, and a sweet little two-headed calf that was born on a local farm and lived for just six days back in 1962.

Maybe that's why the Waterville tourist brochures say the museum is "worth a second look." To see the meteorites, the Popsicle-stick church, the two-headed calf, and other local treasures, stop by the Douglas County Historical Museum, next to Pioneer Park on US 2 in Waterville. Phone (509) 745-8435.

Miniature Marvels
Wenatchee

When he was just sixteen, back in 1900, Jules Charbneau enlisted in the U.S. Navy and was soon serving as an apprentice seaman on the square-rigged sailing ship the USS *Monongahela.* The ship sailed to France, where Charbneau had the opportunity to attend the Paris Exposition and shop for souvenirs. Remembering that his personal space aboard the ship was extremely limited, Charbneau decided to buy miniature items, taking home a delicate jeweled bird, a tiny cross, and a precious petite pipe. He also acquired a lifelong obsession with collecting small things.

By the 1930s Charbneau's collection had grown to about 30,000 items, and he and his family toured the country showing off choice pieces to the public. Venues included New York City's Radio City Music

Hall and the San Francisco Golden Gate International Exhibit on Treasure Island, where more than five million people attended lectures about the collection and lined up to peer into the exhibit cases.

What they saw was tiny and amazing: a ten-piece set of French enameled china furniture, a Chinese bride's sewing chest containing forty-five finely carved pieces, an intricately carved ivory figure of Siamese twins, a filigree table with six legs, a Chinese junk with open windows, and much more.

When Charbneau died in 1968, his daughter Isabella inherited the collection. She continued collecting and traveling around the world, displaying favorite items and lecturing about her tiny treasures. When she could no longer care for the collection, she dismantled it, giving some items to the Ripley's Believe It or Not Museums in various cities around the country.

Because she'd lived in Wenatchee for more than fifty years, Isabella Charbneau-Warren donated many of her favorite miniatures to the Wenatchee Valley Museum and Cultural Center. That batch includes a twenty-nine-figure rickshaw wedding procession that is just a half-inch high, four billiard players complete with cues and balls in a matchbox-size glass case, a Japanese man in a kimono painted on a pea bean, and a 1-inch wooden box containing a candle snuffer, scissors, and tweezers. There's also an oil painting on a grain of rice depicting the raising of the U.S. flag on the island of Iwo Jima, the world's smallest belt, and, most appropriately, a tiny carving made in the image of Jules Charbneau.

Although these items certainly don't take up much display space, the museum is concerned about exposing the more delicate items to too much light. Therefore, only a small portion of the miniatures collection is on view at any one time.

The Charbneau-Warren Miniature Collection is displayed at the Wenatchee Valley Museum and Cultural Center at 127 South Mission Street in Wenatchee. For more information phone (509) 664-3340 or visit www.wenatcheevalleymuseum.com.

HOW ABOUT THEM APPLES?

Wenatchee's tradition of celebrating its connection with the region's apple industry reaches back to the early 1900s, when the local Ladies Musical Club produced the first "Blossom Days" festival. That one-day party involved singing, speeches, maypoles, and baseball. Now more than eighty-five years old and rechristened the Washington State Apple Blossom Festival, this eleven-day extravaganza runs from the last weekend in April through the first weekend in May and includes parades, art exhibits, square dances, an Apple Blossom Run, and a golf tournament. Leading into the festivities is the Mariachi Northwest Festival, which celebrates the Mexican and Latino culture of many of the folks who bring in the apple crop each fall. To get more information about these festivals, phone (509) 662-3616 or log on to www.apple blossom.org.

Perhaps it was all that apple-festing that got Wenatchee residents dreaming of giant apple pies. At some point local officials just couldn't stomach the fact that since 1982 the folks in Chelsfield, England, had held the *Guinness Book of World Records* title for baking the world's largest apple pie. So on August 16, 1997, 800 apple-loving Wenatchee-area volunteers rolled up their sleeves and pre-pared to bake their own record-setting pie.

Here's how they did it:

Two thousand hours went into designing and building the pie pan and the oven. The pan was a rectangular steel behemoth, 44-feet-long by 24-feet-wide and just about a foot deep. The specially designed oven was made of steel tubing wrapped in chicken wire, aluminum foil, and insulation. While the pan and the oven were being built, volunteers set about slicing 37,333 pounds of apples.

The apples were added to more than 3,000 pounds of flour, close to 4,000 pounds of white and brown sugar, 1,227 pounds of shortening, and 100 pounds of cinnamon. A final "pinch" of salt totaled 16 pounds.

All that effort paid off: The completed pie weighed in at 34,438 pounds, several thousand pounds heavier than the one baked by the folks in England, and just three months later a certificate arrived in town from the *Guinness Book of World Records* declaring Wenatchee's apple pie the world's largest. So far, no one seems to have gotten anywhere close to challenging the record.

WORLD'S SHORTEST ST. PATRICK'S DAY PARADE

As it is in many other cities, St. Patrick's Day in Wenatchee is a celebratory affair: People wear green, folks pin on "Kiss Me, I'm Irish" buttons, and the line of floats, bands, and costumed revelers waiting anxiously to march in the parade stretches out for blocks. But if you blink, stand in the wrong spot, or take just a wee bit too long to drink that green beer at the pub, you might miss the parade entirely. That's because downtown Wenatchee's St. Patrick's Day Parade route is just one block long.

No one seems to mind. They've been celebrating St. Patrick's Day in Wenatchee this way for more than ten years, handing out prizes for everything from the wackiest float to the person who traveled the farthest to participate in the parade. Erin Go Short!

Apples in Flight

Wenatchee

Wenatchee's love affair with apples is extremely well documented in the multimedia Apple Exhibit gallery at the Wenatchee Valley Museum and Cultural Center. Designed to resemble the inside of an apple-packing shed, the exhibit includes a wall filled with colorful apple crate labels, sporting company names such as William Tell and Yum Yum, and an operational vintage apple-packing line, complete with apple wiper, sorting table, and an extraordinary apple-sizing machine.

This amazing catapult contraption separates a batch of apples into bins according to weight, operating pretty much like a baseball pitching machine. Be sure to ask the receptionist at the front desk to get some-one to turn the machine on for you. In a real apple-packing shed, once the apples were separated by catapult, they'd be wrapped in tissue paper and hand packed into wooden boxes according to size.

The Wenatchee Valley Museum and Cultural Center is at 127 South Mission Street in Wenatchee. For more information, call (509) 664 3340 or log on to www.wenatcheevalleymuseum.com.

And the folks at the Washington State Apple Commission offer these appealing apple anecdotes to augment your apple appetite:

- More than half of the apples grown for fresh eating in the United States come from Washington State.
- One apple has five grams of fiber.
- Each American eats less than twenty pounds of fresh apples annually. In Europe, they eat closer to forty-six pounds per person each year.
- Between ten and twelve billion apples are picked each year. Each apple is picked by hand. No harvest machines help out with the task.

- Washington apple harvest season runs from mid-August through early November.
- In order of harvest, Washington's major apple varieties include Gala, Jonagold, Golden Delicious, Red Delicious, Braeburn, Granny Smith, Fuji, Cameo, and Pink Lady.
- The only apple native to North America is the crabapple.

Source: Washington State Apple Commission, www.bestapples.com

WACKY WENATCHEE

If you do miss the petite St. Patrick's Day Parade, don't panic. There are some other area events that are just as wacky, and that last just a bit longer.

During the December Flake Festival, for example, each entrant in a parade that wends its way through downtown Wenatchee must be lighted in some manner. "You can light up the dog, string lights on Grandpa's Chevy, turn yourself into a walking Christmas tree, or pretend to be Rudolph's nose. Just as long as you're lit," says a local organizer.

Dummies get ready.

And each January, during the "Dummy Downhill" at the nearby Mission Ridge Ski & Board Resort (7500 Mission Ridge Road), costumed mannequins are launched from the hill. Registration forms lay out "Dummy Specs," which require that all dummies be on skis or a snowboard, be of human or animal form, and weigh in at under one hundred pounds. In addition, the rules prohibit motorization or explosives, steel beams, or other heavy objects. Dummies (and their creators) can win in several categories, including Most Creative and Most Likely to Survive.

For more information contact the Wenatchee Valley Convention & Visitor's Bureau at (800) 572-7753 or visit www.wenatcheevalley.org or www.missionridge.com.

Who are you calling dummy? Let's take it outside.

SOUTH AND SOUTHWEST

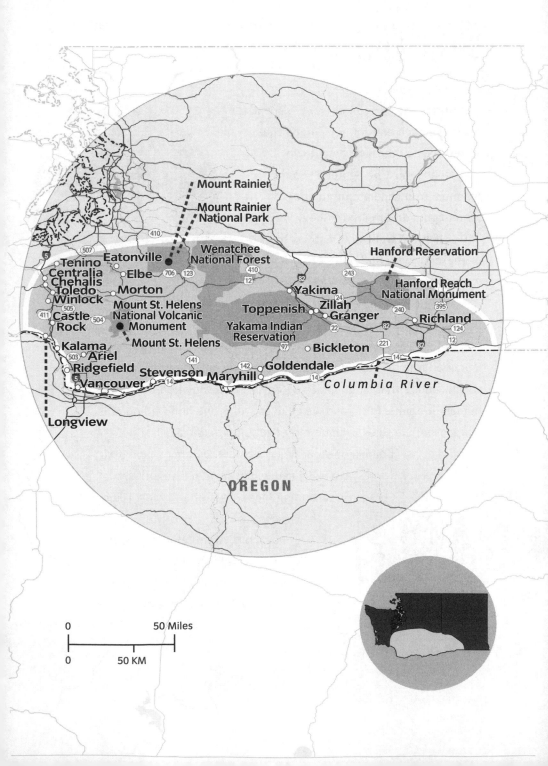

Mount Rainier

Mount Rainier National Park

Wenatchee National Forest

Hanford Reservation

Eatonville

Tenino
Centralia
Chehalis
Toledo
Winlock

Elbe

Morton

Yakima

Hanford Reach National Monument

Castle Rock

Mount St. Helens National Volcanic Monument

Toppenish

Zillah
Granger

Richland

Mount St. Helens

Yakama Indian Reservation

Kalama
Ariel

Bickleton

Ridgefield

Stevenson

Goldendale

Vancouver

Maryhill

Columbia River

Longview

OREGON

0   50 Miles

0   50 KM

SOUTH AND SOUTHWEST

Encompassing the Columbia River Gorge, the Yakima Valley, and "Volcano Country" (Mount Rainier, Mount St. Helens, and Mount Adams), Washington's south and southwest regions offer up plenty of jaw-dropping destinations and amusing attractions.

While traveling this area, I especially enjoyed learning about the world's largest ginseng root, Longview's commitment to a bridge built especially for squirrels, and the laws enacted to protect Sasquatch, a creature that no one has ever actually laid eyes on, but plenty of folks insist exists.

Residents of southwest Washington don't just keep their eyes peeled for Sasquatch: Ever since the early 1970s, they've been on the lookout for D. B. Cooper, or more specifically, his cash. On November 24, 1971, Dan Cooper, or someone calling himself by that name, set out on a Northwest Airlines flight from Portland to Seattle. En route he handed a flight attendant a note saying that he would set off the bomb in his briefcase unless the plane touched down in Seattle and took off again once Cooper was given four parachutes and $200,000 in cash.

Those demands were met, and Cooper insisted that the plane head south with both its flaps and landing gear down. Then, somewhere over southwestern Washington, Cooper lowered the airplane's rear stairs and jumped out. Despite an exhaustive manhunt and a flurry of unconfirmed sightings, Cooper has never been heard from since. Most people believe he didn't survive his escape, especially since the only traces found of the marked money Cooper took with him were a few packs of bills discovered along the banks of the Columbia River in 1980.

Cooper Caper
Ariel

The hijacker known as D. B. Cooper may still be at large. And so is most of the $200,000 he took with him when he parachuted out of an airplane somewhere over southwestern Washington—some say near the logging town of Ariel—on Thanksgiving eve in 1971.

Cooper's daring escape, and all that missing and possibly unmarked money, has made Cooper somewhat of a cult hero. So beginning in 1976, and continuing each year around Thanksgiving, the Ariel General Store and Tavern memorializes D. B. Cooper's plunge with a party. Festivities include a look-alike contest, a special D. B. Cooper stew, and the singing of the D. B. Cooper song. Store owner Dona Elliott says hundreds of folks come from far and wide to join in the party. Throughout the year, many others drop by to visit the "Cooper Corner," filled with maps and articles about the notorious unsolved hijacking case.

And what if the real D. B. Cooper showed up for the party? Well, the statute of limitations on his crime ran out in 1976, but the IRS would still like to talk with him about the considerable amount of taxes and penalties he still owes on that $200,000. No doubt the FBI still has plenty of questions as well.

The Ariel Store and Tavern is located in Ariel at 288 Merwin Village Road, 10 miles east of Woodland on State Route 503. For more information call the Ariel Store at (360) 225-7126.

Somewhere over the Rainbow

Bickleton

With a population hovering at just around one hundred, the wheat-farming community of Bickleton is a small town that crows proudly about its title of Bluebird Capital of the World.

Back in the mid-1960s, Jess and Elva Brinkerhoff started putting up bluebird houses in and around Bickleton after they noticed a pair of bluebirds searching around for a home. They lent a hand by nailing a one-gallon tin can to a tree. The bluebirds seemed to like that, so the Brinker-hoffs went home and started building traditional bird-houses with gusto.

Bickleton's 2,000 blue-roofed birdhouses help make Bickleton the Bluebird Capital of the World.

Thirty years later, more than 2,000 fence posts and trees across 150 square miles of Klickitat County sported the Brinkerhoffs' white wooden birdhouses with bright blue roofs. Word apparently spread through the bluebird community, because thousands of Blue Mountain bluebirds and red-breasted Western bluebirds literally began to flock to the area each February and stay around until October, taking up residence in the lovely little homes.

After Elva died in 1985, Jess turned the task of building and maintaining the bluebird houses over to the Bluebird Brigade, a group of area volunteers who build and post more birdhouses and clean up after the flock of feathered visitors takes flight each fall.

You can see Bickleton's birdhouses year-round, but it's best to visit after Valentine's Day, when the male and female bluebirds that went south for the winter in gender-separated flocks reunite for spring mating season.

To get to Bickleton, head north from State Route 14 at Roosevelt. You should start seeing birdhouses on the fence posts along the highway. In the tiny town of Bickleton, next to the post office, you'll find a large birdhouse-shaped memorial thanking Jess and Elva Brinkerhoff for bringing the bluebirds to town. For more information call (509) 773-7060 or check the town's Web site, www.bickleton.org.

Ride 'em Cowpoke

Bickleton

Ever since 1910 the folks in and around Bickleton have gathered
together on the weekend before Father's Day at Cleveland Pioneer Park
for the Alder Creek Pioneer Picnic and Rodeo. Locals and visitors alike
are welcome to participate in all the festivities, which include cowboy
breakfasts, a Saturday night country dance, bull riding, cow milking,
barrel racing, and all manner of
classic roping and riding
events.

Kids of all ages wait all year for a chance to ride on Bickleton's 1905 Herschell-Spillman carousel.

For some people, though, riding a bucking horse or roping a steer just isn't their style. Happily, those folks can saddle up something a little tamer. Well, a lot tamer. The town of Bickleton owns a rare 1905 Herschell-Spillman carousel that's usually kept locked up in an old bank vault. It's brought out of storage once each year, during the weekend of the annual rodeo.

The carousel, a two-row track machine with no overhead connections, is one of the oldest in the West and one of only three of its type still in operation. It was purchased from the Oaks Amusement Park in Portland, Oregon, in the late 1920s, and local volunteers have been slowly and lovingly restoring the twenty-four wooden ponies and four carriages over the years.

Before there were power lines that reached out to the fairgrounds, the carousel was run first by an electric generator, then by an International Harvester tractor engine. Now an electric motor the size of a thirty-gallon water tank keeps the antique moving.

The Pioneer Picnic and Rodeo is held each year on the second weekend in June. The rodeo grounds are located in Cleveland, about 4 miles west of Bickleton. For more information call (509) 773-7060.

Bluebird Inn
Bickleton

If you find yourself anywhere near tiny "downtown" Bickleton, be sure to stop in at the Bluebird Inn. Opened in 1882 and one of two taverns claiming to be the oldest saloon in Washington State (the other is "The Brick" in Roslyn), the Bluebird Inn at 105 E Market Street is a popular and somewhat quirky town hangout that miraculously, some say, has survived multiple ownership changes and several fires that have swept through town.

The tavern, which at one time doubled as the town's barbershop, still has its original wood floor and an original 1903 Brunswick pool table "that the folks at Brunswick would love to have in their own collection," says Ada Ruth Whitmore over at Bickleton's Whoop-n-Holler Museum, "but I don't think they're going to get their hands on it anytime soon." "Decorated" (we choose that word carefully) with wagon wheels hanging from the ceiling, deer antlers, board paintings, and a steady clientele of colorful locals, the tavern also has an old card table on hand that has a half circle cut into it that allowed a previous owner to reach for poker and pinochle cards over his large belly.

We'll Just Keep That Too

Bickleton

Just 11 miles south of Bickleton is the rambling Whoop-n-Holler Ranch and Museum, a treasure trove of antiques, curios, whatnots, and exotic memorabilia, all looked after by Lawrence and Ada Ruth Whitmore, a charming and enthusiastic duo now in their seventies.

The couple grew up in this area, and their families homesteaded around these parts in the late 1800s. Their marriage, in 1947, came with a lifelong commitment to keeping all sorts of family heirlooms and to collecting pretty much anything that seemed intriguing.

And collect they have. Lawrence Whitmore has filled a large barn with Model T Fords, antique pickup trucks, horse-drawn wagons, and other vintage modes of transportation, including the 1927 Studebaker he drove when he was courting Ada Ruth.

A 1900 schoolhouse and several other buildings scattered around the property are filled with pioneer memorabilia, historic photographs, the tin tub the couple used during their first few years of marriage, an "electric" lunch box, and thousands of other "artifacts" that entwine the Whitmore's family tree with the history of east Klickitat County.

Stop by and ask how the Whitmores got that hand-carved doll furniture, the antique organ, the chest of drawers that turns into a bed, that sleigh hearse complete with wicker body basket, the brass bell from the Methodist church in Mabton, or that collection of dubious home remedies, and you'll be treated to an entertaining afternoon of stories that bring local history to life.

The Whoop-n-Holler Museum, on East Road just south of Bickleton, is open May through September. For directions and hours of operation, call (509) 896-2344. *Note:* The museum will be closed for most of 2007, while the Whitmores take a much-deserved break and get out on the road for some touring of their own. "We're getting on in years," says a still very perky-sounding Ada Ruth, "and we want to see what sort of stuff other folks have been collecting and showing in their museums."

Thar She Blows!
Castle Rock

Before 1980 Castle Rock was a classic Northwest fishing and logging town. Timber, smelt, sawmills, and pulp and paper operations kept folks busy. The town was also one of the places tourists passed through on their way to visit scenic Mount St. Helens.

All that changed with the mountain's May 18, 1980, eruption.

As one local resident remembers it, "When the mountain blew, ash turned the Toutle River thick as pancake batter and made the water so hot that fish got cooked while they swam!" Bridges, homes, and area businesses were destroyed, and mud and debris from the Cowlitz River overflowed the banks, covering the town's high school football and track field, the motorcycle track, and the fairgrounds. In the aftermath, giant banks of lights burned around the clock while the Army Corps of

Engineers worked to dredge the ash and the gunk out of the rivers and to set things back in order.

Castle Rock (its motto is "Where Mount St. Helens Happened") uses a small exhibit hall to tell the story of how the eruption of the mountain changed the town. Details on the "premountain" days are here too, from the early Cowlitz Indian era to the logging days, when area timber workers brought home more than eighty world championship titles in events such as speed climbing, tree topping, women's log rolling, axe throwing, and Jack-and-Jill bucking.

The main attraction is definitely the ways in which the center shows the impact of the eruption. Inspect the "before and after" mountain photos, leaf through the scrapbook of newspaper clippings documenting the eruption events, and shake your head in wonder at what's left of a giant tree splintered by the force of Mount St. Helens.

To get a unique "you are there" feel for the event, pick up one of the red telephone handsets on the back wall. You'll hear the actual radio transmissions that went back and forth between 911 dispatchers and the police when the mountain really got going.

To visit the Castle Rock Exhibit Hall, take exit 49 from Interstate 5 and then follow State Route 504 west into town. For more information phone (360) 274-6603 or visit http://cicastle-rock.wa.us.

Art Yard
Centralia

Retired art instructor Richard Tracy says that he doesn't make a living from his art. Instead, he tells visitors to his art-filled yard in downtown Centralia, "I live for my art."

No doubt he does. Tracy, who has adopted the name Richart (as in "rich in art") is an unusual fellow with an unusual definition of art. Some people call him a strange and eccentric character. Others compare him to visionary artist Howard Finster. But everyone agrees that Tracy's work is a wonder to behold.

Styrofoam is the main ingredient in this art-filled yard in Centralia.

SOUTH AND SOUTHWEST

In 1985 Tracy began building abstract sculptures out of Styrofoam and placing them in his front yard. Later, his palette expanded to include other scavenged materials, such as plastics, metal, wire, and rubber. Now Tracy's spires and other quirky constructions completely engulf his home.

Tracy's "Art Yard," as this bizarre collection of artwork is affectionately called, more than stands out on Centralia's main street, which is otherwise dotted with historic murals and lovingly restored late-nineteenth-century homes and buildings. Because drivers just naturally slow down (or screech to a stop) when they come upon his art-filled yard, Tracy keeps it open to the public throughout the summer and by appointment the rest of the year. Most of the time, Tracy watches his visitors and their reactions to his artwork from a spot in his house above the yard. Sometimes he'll open the window to make a comment of his own, or to chat.

Tracy is such an unusual character that he was recently profiled in a film documentary, in which we learn how important the number five is to his life. Visitors to his house are asked to show up only in groups of five, tours of his yard last no more than five minutes, he gives fifty-five-minute art classes, and his work sells for five dollars.

Richard Tracy's Art Yard, at 203 M Street in downtown Centralia, is easily visible from the street. Centralia is just a mile from I-5, at exit 82.

You can try calling ahead for an appointment at (360) 736-7990, but be forewarned: Tracy says he's better with the written word and his art than he is chatting on the phone.

WAS BIGFOOT REALLY AFOOT?

Some kind of big, hairy, and extremely shy creature lives in the Washington woods. Thing is, no one knows exactly what sort of creature it is or if it actually exists.

That hasn't stopped folks from naming it, and it hasn't stopped believers from insisting they've found evidence that Sasquatch or Bigfoot, as the creature has been named, does indeed rumble through the Northwest backcountry.

Northwest Native American tribes have centuries-old legends about a mysterious forest creature and its powers. Modern-day tabloids regularly claim to have the latest gossip about the beast. And a growing network of "creature believers" returns from weekend jaunts into the forest with what they claim is film footage, plaster footprint impressions, hair samples, and the occasional "dropping" left behind by the giant, hairy, manlike being.

There's even an official society that tracks Bigfoot sightings and tries to authenticate gathered evidence. That society, the Bigfoot Field Researchers Organization, has records of Sasquatch sightings in every state except Delaware, Hawaii, and Rhode Island, but with 263 reported sightings, Washington State tops the list.

While legends about a forest Sasquatch reach back to the 1800s, folks didn't get all fired up about a modern-day Bigfoot until 1958, when a bulldozer operator in California discovered unusual 16-inch footprints at his work site. In November 2002, however, after Sasquatch hunter Ray Wallace died in Centralia, his family revealed that it was Wallace who had put those footprints there in the first place. They even claim to have the giant carved alder "feet" that Wallace used to make the footprints.

"He did it for the joke," his nephew told newspapers, "and then he was afraid to tell anybody because they'd be so mad at him."

The revelation doesn't seem to faze Bigfoot believers, who say they'll continue to search the woods for the mysterious creature and to report their findings to the Bigfoot Field Researchers Organization at www.bfro.net.

Jade Jaws
Chehalis

Basil Mulford was a rock hound. His bad back prevented him from going out to dig for rocks, so he built up his rock collection by buying and trading choice specimens of agate, jade, and other collectible rocks with other enthusiasts. Staying out of the field was just fine with Mulford because it left lots more time for his specialty lapidary creations.

Mulford didn't just use his rocks to make things like paperweights and bolo ties. He mixed rocks with tiny lightbulbs, parts of old television sets, clock timers, and all manner of things he'd find around his house. Then he'd show off his creations at rock swaps.

One year he made a Christmas tree tie festooned with slices of gemstones that allowed the hues from a tiny motorized color wheel to shine through. Another time he showed up with a clock that had neither hands nor numbers, just twelve agates inset at the spots where the hours would be and a dozen minute-signifying rocks attached to a piece of glass. Lights behind the rocks marked the time, and a brass bell rang at the top of each hour. Mulford was especially proud of his all-rock hand organ that was built inside the hull of a television set and wired up to turn on a different light each time a note was played.

The Mulford creation that got folks chattering, though, is the one that proved, once and for all, that the collector really did have rocks in his head. When Mulford's dentures began to wear out, he asked a dental technician friend to help him make a one-of-a-kind upper plate embedded with agates, jade, and a sparkling red tigereye from his collection.

Basil Mulford died in 1993, but his dentures live on at the Lewis County Historical Museum at 599 NW Front Way in Chehalis. From I-5, take exit 79 and follow the signs to the museum. For more information phone (360) 748-0831 or visit www.lewiscountymuseum.org.

Slug Fest
Eatonville

With their bright yellow bodies dotted with brown spots, banana slugs look like, well, like little bananas. The second-largest slugs in the world, they can grow up to a foot long (There have been reports of foot-long ones!) and, when they're on the move, stretch out even farther. These shell-less mollusks can be a bit icky, especially if you happen to step on one in the woods, but they're also native to the Northwest. Which is why, for the past ten years, the folks at the Northwest Trek Wildlife Park have been happy to host a slime-filled Slug Fest in honor of the banana slug each June.

Festival highlights include the singing of a "Slug Anthem" and the running of the Human Slug Races, in which contestants encased in brown tubular "slug suits" wiggle, squiggle, and squirm their way toward a finish line. In addition to the races, Slug Fest participants can attend Slug School and earn a degree in Slugology by attending classes in slug anatomy, slug feeding habits, and slug identification. Graduate degrees from the School of Slime can also be earned by those who choose to delve deeper into the dank, damp darkness of slug life.

Slime-school scholars can learn, for example, that a slug can eat three times its weight in a single day, that it leaves behind a scent that it can follow home after dark, and that a slug has more teeth than a shark.

Want to learn more? The Slug Fest is held each June at the Northwest Trek Wildlife Park Center, a 715-acre park with a large free-roaming area that's home to more than 200 North American animals, including bears, bison, wolverines, wolves, foxes, snakes, salamanders, bobcats, cougars, and more. It's located at 11610 Trek Drive E in Eatonville, near Mount Rainier, about 35 miles southeast of Tacoma. For hours, admission fees, and directions, call (360) 832-6117 or visit www.nwtrek.org.

SLUG ANTHEM

(to the tune of the
U.S. National Anthem)

Slime to the finish line.

Slugs are gooey
Oozing when it rains
Leaving slimy trails neat
'Cause they don't have any feet
Slugs are pokey and slow
They don't get up and go
Slugs sit and stay
Slimin' round the whole day
And slugs e-at and eat
Lettuce plants and beets
What's left when they leave?
Lots of dirt bare and clean
Slugs are slimy. Slugs are yellow.
They are ever so mellow
Slugs are sticky slimy too.
We love them, you will, too!

(Courtesy Northwest Trek Wildlife Park)

Metal Merriment
Elbe

If you're heading out on State Route 706, on your way to Paradise Lodge and Mount Rainier National Park, keep an eye out for Aspen Zoe. You really can't miss her: She's that 18-foot-tall giraffe made from recycled scrap metal by the side of the road. And she's just one of the magical creations in Daniel Klennert's sculpture park, a four-acre wonderland he's dubbed Ex Nihilo, which is Latin for "something created out of nothing."

Klennert is a mechanic and self-taught artist who admits to falling in love at a young age with old gears, driftwood, stones, discarded metal, and other "junk." He used to live in Seattle, but says he ran out of room for his oversize artwork in the city and so headed to the country, where he cleared a piece of land so his sculptures could "run free."

That was in 1998, and since then he's been busy turning all sorts of "nothings" into more than forty wild, weird, whimsical, and in some cases, X-rated, sculptural "somethings"—everything from fish and other sea creatures to motorcycles, bicycles, dinosaurs, and musicians armed with scrap-metal guitars and trumpets. One of his favorite creations is a Sasquatch sculpture made as an homage to the rarely seen and, some say, mythical creature who prowls the northwest woods. "Someday," says Klennert, "I imagine looking out the window and seeing a 'real' Sasquatch visiting my driftwood Sasquatch."

Scrappy Sasquatch.

Klennert, who will happily take a break from welding another wonder to chat with visitors, welcomes passersby to stop by for self-guided tours of the Ex Nihilo sculpture park. Admission is free, but donations are accepted. The park is located on State Route 706, about 3 miles east of Elbe and 14 miles from the west entrance to Mount Rainier National Park. Klennert leaves the gate open from April through October, but during the winter visitors are welcome to hike in from the road. For more information visit www.danielklennert.com or call (360) 569-2280.

Eye on the Universe
Goldendale

Amateur astronomers are used to reaching for the sky, so in the mid-1960s, when four self-taught astronomers from Vancouver, Washington, decided to pool their knowledge and resources to build a $75,000 telescope from scratch, they just assumed they'd succeed.

It took a while, but not only did M. W. McConnell, O. W. VanderVeldon, John Marshall, and Don Connor succeed in constructing a 24-inch Cassegrain reflecting telescope for less than $3,000, they also set in motion the creation of what is now a state park housing one of the nation's largest publicly accessible telescopes.

Not long after they started their project, the astronomers realized that Vancouver wouldn't be a good home for their telescope. There were too many city lights and too many cloudy nights. Drier and hillier Goldendale, to the east, seemed like a much better prospect. So the plucky astronomers offered their telescope to the citizens of Goldendale. All the town had to do was locate a site and build an observatory.

No small feat, but the folks in Goldendale came through, and the Goldendale Observatory opened to the public in 1973. Just a few years later, the observatory gained national prominence when it was designated the official headquarters of the National Astronomical League for the total eclipse of February 26, 1979. The Goldendale location was not only the closest place on the eclipse path to the population centers of Portland and Seattle, it was the only city in the eclipse path with a telescope and an observatory. And because so many people wanted to view the eclipse that was scheduled to last for less than two and a half minutes, the telescope was turned over to NBC-TV so that network cameras could broadcast the event on a live telecast.

Today the Washington State Parks and Recreation Commission runs the Goldendale Observatory as a state park. A 20-foot-diameter dome houses that original homemade telescope, and public sky-gazing programs are offered throughout the year. The observatory hill offers great views of the universe at night and equally inspiring views of the countryside during the day.

Hours at the Goldendale Observatory State Park vary by season. For more information and directions to Goldendale Observatory State Park, call (509) 773-3141 or check the park's Web site, www.perr.com/gosp.html.

Prehistoric Welcome Wagon
Granger

Granger bills itself as a culturally diverse community "Where Dinosaurs Roam." They're not talking about the folks from the local old-age home. The dinosaurs dotting the Granger landscape are made of wire mesh and concrete, and each *Brontosaurus, Triceratops,* and *Tyrannosaurus rex* has a shiny coat of automotive paint.

Where did these creatures come from? Well, back in 1958 tusks, teeth, and assorted bones from a woolly mammoth were discovered in an abandoned clay pit near Granger. So in the mid-1990s town officials digging for a tourism theme decided to play up the town's prehistoric past. Public works crews were assigned to build dinosaurs and scatter them around town. The response was so positive that now Granger is home to close to two dozen dinosaurs, some almost 12 feet tall. There's one that looks like it's busting its way through the wall of the city's public works building, a few that live out in front of city hall, and a mother with a nest of baby dinosaurs by the library. And over in Dinosaur Park there are climbable creatures and a pterosaur in the middle of the man-made pond.

Dinosaurs rule in Granger.

Drive around town and you'll find even more dinosaurs dawdling in many of the city's small parks as well as shops and services that have adopted a dino-theme, including Jurassic Java Espresso and a car wash/laundromat called Dino-Wash. And early each June dinosaur fans are invited to come by and help the public works department create a brand new dinosaur for the collection during the town's Dino-in-a-Day Festival.

Determined to take a Dino-tour? Granger is located 23 miles south of Yakima at the intersection of Highway 223 and Interstate 82, at exit 58. The Dinosaur Park is located at the south end of Main Street and Highway 223. A large map noting the locations of all the town's dinosaurs is located at the entrance to the east end of town, at the corner of Bailey Avenue and Highway 223.

For more information about the dinosaurs and the annual Dino-in-a-Day Festival, call the Granger Chamber of Commerce at (509) 854-7304 or see their Web site, www.grangerchamber.org.

Hot History
Hanford

In 1943 the top-secret Manhattan Project was created in order to facilitate the production of the atomic bomb for use in World War II. Scientists needed either uranium or plutonium for the project, but it was unclear which substance could be produced quickly and in large enough quantities. So it was decided to produce both: uranium in Tennessee, plutonium in Washington State, at the Hanford Engineer Works.

To make way for the plutonium production plant, the remote rural communities of Richland, White Bluffs, and Hanford, 560 square miles in all, were disincorporated and all the towns' residents were evacuated. New residents—51,000 of them—were brought in to work in secret, building three plutonium production facilities on the banks of the Columbia River to produce the plutonium used in the atomic bomb that was dropped on Nagasaki, Japan. (Uranium from Tennessee was used in the bomb that was dropped on Hiroshima.) These plants later played a major role in the nuclear buildup of the Cold War, but by 1988 plutonium production at Hanford was discontinued. The site, however, is still the home of a Washington Public Power Supply System (WPPSS) nuclear plant.

All that plutonium production left behind fifty-four million gallons of radioactive waste, and today several government branches are involved in the world's largest environmental cleanup project, spending more than $1 billion a year to clean up one of the world's most toxic spots.

You cannot visit the old plutonium plants (would you really want to?), and since September 11, 2001, all public tours of the area have been discontinued. However, you can learn more about the history of Hanford and the cleanup efforts under way by visiting www.hanford.gov.

ALPHABET HOUSES

The thousands of people arriving in town to work at the Hanford Site needed places to live. Fast. So the government hired Spokane architect G. A. Pehrson to design easy-to-erect apartments, dormitories, duplexes, and single-family homes. Pehrson gave each design a letter of the alphabet, and the structures came to be known as "alphabet houses." Residents who later purchased the houses have made modifications, adding porches, entryways, and other features, but the basic styles can still be spotted around town.

For those not lucky enough to take up residence in one of the alphabet homes, there were trailers. A small, silver travel trailer offered no more than 150 square feet of living space, and at the height of Hanford's operations, each trailer accommodated an average of 3.7 people. The Hanford Construction Camp had spots for more than 3,600 trailers; at the time it was the world's largest trailer camp.

Elvis Slept Here
Kalama

On September 4, 1962, Elvis Presley and an eight-member entourage spent the night in Kalama's only motel. Presley, who'd told his bodyguards that he wanted to stay in a small, out-of-the-way place, snoozed in room 219 (or maybe it was 220, it's a suite) of what is now the otherwise nondescript Kalama River Inn. He also had a meal in a local restaurant.

The King was kind enough to pose for the pictures that now hang behind the motel's front desk and to sign more than 150 autographs for the folks in town before heading on up the road to Seattle, where they were waiting for him on the set of the film *It Happened at the World's Fair*. Not long after Elvis moved on, actor Sebastian Cabot (he played Mr. French on TV's *Family Affair*) was spotted wandering around town, but according to one of the few people who recognized him, Cabot's visit barely caused a ripple. Maybe everyone was still all shook up from seeing Elvis.

We suspect they've changed the mattress since Presley was here, but if you want to try sleeping like the King in Kalama, you'll find the Kalama River Inn at 602 NE Frontage Road; phone (360) 673-1211.

Tallest Totem
Kalama

If Elvis had wandered around Kalama a bit, he might have come upon a 140-foot totem pole lying on the ground. Later listed in the *Guinness Book of World Records* as the tallest one-piece totem in the world, the pole was supposed to be something Elvis and others could marvel at while visiting the 1962 World's Fair in Seattle. Unfortunately, the pole didn't get finished in time.

In fact, Native American artist Don Lelooska, who was commissioned to carve the pole out of a 700-year-old western red cedar tree, never did get it finished. Instead, the pole lay rotting on the ground for twelve years until it was rescued by a group of local citizens. They applied finishing paint and arranged to have the tall totem, along with three others carved and completed by Lelooska, erected on land near the river owned by the Port of Kalama.

The tallest one-piece totem pole towers over a tiny park in Kalama.

Port officials are mighty proud of that totem. They consider it a land-mark, and they get a bit testy if anyone questions whether or not it is still the world's tallest. "Some folks in Canada claim they have the tallest totem, but we don't believe them," one official declared. "We're sticking with our claim."

Towering over a lovely little park, the totems are easily visible from the highway. If you'd like to have a closer look, head for Kalama's Marine Park, near the river on the west side of I-5, at exit 30.

Squirrel Bridge

Longview

In 1963 local builder Amos Peters became concerned about the squir-rels outside his office window. He and his coworkers would often put out treats for the squirrels that lived in a nearby park, but to their hor-ror, some of the squirrels trying to cross the street to chow down ended up getting mowed down and flattened by passing cars.

After finding a dead squirrel still clutching a nut, Peters flew into action. He thought that perhaps a tree-level sky bridge that reached over the busy thoroughfare might help keep the squirrels out of harm's way. So, with a committee of equally concerned local businesspeople, he went before the city council, seeking permission to proceed with his plan. The council gave its blessing and even came up with a name for the project: Nutty Narrows.

Several bright-eyed and bushy-tailed local architects, structural engi-neers, and builders put their heads together and built a 60-foot sky bridge out of aluminum and lengths of fire hose. The final bill, $1,000, seemed to be money well spent. City officials say squirrels started using the bridge right away and some were even seen "escorting their young and teaching them the ropes."

Soon after the story of the squirrel bridge made the papers and the *Guinness Book of World Records,* squirrel lovers from around the world were sending fan mail and bags full of nuts to project organizer Amos Peters.

After twenty years of heavy squirrel traffic, the bridge was worn out. So in 1983 Peters spearheaded an upgrade of Nutty Narrows. The subsequent rededication of the world's only bridge for squirrels was attended by 300 children and well-known cartoon chipmunks Chip 'n' Dale.

Amos Peters died in 1984. To honor both his memory and his dedication to squirrel safety, the city placed a 10-foot-tall wooden sculpture of a squirrel between the city's library and the squirrel sky bridge.

You can visit the statue and peer up at the bridge on Olympia Way, in downtown Longview, near the Longview Public Library. For more information phone (360) 423-8400.

No need for squirrels in Longview to cross the busy street; they have their own sky bridge.

Would You Wear That?

Maryhill

In 1907 Northwest entrepreneur Sam Hill purchased 7,000 acres of land along the Columbia River for a Quaker agricultural colony that was never built. Hill also commissioned a massive three-story poured-concrete "country getaway" in the area, but he lost interest in that too.

Hill's friend Loie Fuller, the flamboyant pioneer of modern dance known in Paris as the "Fairy of Light," convinced Hill to turn the unfinished ranch house into a museum, and Fuller's friend Queen Marie of Romania

After World War II, Parisian fashion designers used mannequins instead of models to show off their latest creations.

agreed to come over for the dedication in 1926. Unfortunately, after Queen Marie made a much publicized thirty-seven-day train trip across the United States, she arrived at Maryhill only to discover that after ten years of "work," the museum was little more than a concrete shell!

The museum finally did open—in 1940—and today the Maryhill Museum of Art, a castlelike chateau overlooking the Columbia River Gorge, is a showcase for an eclectic array of collections ranging from royal Romanian artifacts and Native American baskets and beadwork to antique chess sets and sculpture by French master Auguste Rodin.

Perhaps the most curious collection at Maryhill is the Théâtre de la Mode. This rare set of miniature French fashion mannequins, each one-third human size and made of wire, was created by the top Paris costume houses after World War II in an effort to reclaim their status as *the* arbiters of fashion. Dressed in outfits created by the major Parisian designers of the day, the finely attired mannequins toured Europe and then the United States, wearing stunning accessories and accompanied by specially composed incidental music and sets.

Unfortunately, at the end of the tour the collection was left jumbled up and abandoned in a San Francisco department store. Years later, sugar heiress and Maryhill trustee Alma Spreckels arranged for Maryhill to provide shelter, but by then no one knew for sure which tiny shoes went with what finely tailored small outfit.

The story has a happy ending: In the 1980s a professor working on a fashion-related documentary rediscovered the collection and helped arrange for a total restoration in Paris. The clothes were cleaned and pressed, the hats blocked, the shoes shined, and each tiny ensemble put back together. Now the Théâtre de la Mode shines as one of the gems at the Maryhill Museum of Art on U.S. Highway 97, about 8 miles south of Goldendale. For hours, directions, and additional information, call (509) 773-3733 or log on to www.maryhillmuseum.org.

Stonehenge Replica
Maryhill

Four miles east of the Maryhill Museum of Art, you'll find a full-size (though not exact) replica of England's neolithic Stonehenge. Sam Hill ordered this monument built as a World War I memorial for the fallen soldiers from Klickitat County, Washington, and it is the first memorial built in this country to honor the heroes of that war. Like the museum, construction of the memorial took a long time. Although the altar stone was dedicated on July 4, 1918, the memorial wasn't completed until 1929. Today the Klickitat County soldiers who died in World War II, Korea, and Vietnam are also honored here.

Had Hill gotten his facts straight, he might not have embarked on this project at all. According to museum records, Hill, a Quaker pacifist, was erroneously told that the original Stonehenge was used as a sacrificial

Stonehenge replica at Maryhill.

site. Believing this, Hill announced that he was constructing the replica as a reminder that "humanity is still being sacrificed to the god of war."

If you'd like to pay your respects to Maryhill founder Sam Hill, you'll find his crypt directly south of the Stonehenge replica, overlooking the Columbia River.

Hill's Stonehenge is located 1 mile east of the junction of US 97 and State Route 14, 4 miles east of the Maryhill Museum of Art. For more information call (509) 773-3733 or log on to www.maryhillmuseum.org.

Chain Saw Savvy
Morton

At one time, the Northwest woods were filled with loggers and logging camps. After spending weeks at a time chopping down trees, dragging them out of the woods, and sending the timber off to become straight-edged lumber at the sawmills, what did these woodsmen do? They'd get together with lumberjacks from other camps and compete against each other to see who could chop, top, climb, and saw the fastest.

Although there are fewer loggers at work today, folks who work in the woods keep that "I'm a better chopper" tradition alive with timber festivals held in many Northwest communities.

All the events are fun and, for urban dwellers, darn educational, but only four competitions in the state are officially sanctioned by the American Lumberjack Association. Those festivals, held in Kettle Falls each June, in Longview each July, in Morton each August, and in Hoquiam each September, feature events that range from chopping a huge log in half to climbing a tree and slicing off the top of it. All this while a timer is running and contestants have sharp blades in their hands.

At Morton's annual Loggers' Jubilee, held in the second week of August, contestants compete for cash prizes in events titled Springboard, Obstacle Buck, Stock Saw, Hot Saw, and Speed Climb. For non-loggers there are lawn mower and bed races, a parade, fireworks, and fishing. They even crown a Jubilee queen and a court of princesses.

To find out more about the Morton Loggers' Jubilee, call (360) 496-6362 or log on to www.loggersjubilee.com.

Loggers at play.

SEARCHING FOR MORE SAWING?

The Kettle Falls logging competition is held as part of the Kettle Falls Town and Country Days each year in the first weekend in June. For more information, phone (509) 738-2300 or visit www.kettlefalls.com.

The city of Longview holds its annual logging competition during the Fourth of July "Go Fourth Festival"; (360) 578-2553; www.go fourthfestival.org.

In Hoquiam, the Loggers Playday is held each September. For dates and more information, phone (360) 532-5700 or visit www .graysharbortourism.com.

Spirit of a Cranky Man
Mount St. Helens

Until it blew 1,312 feet off its top in 1980, Mount St. Helens was Washington State's fifth-highest peak. Now only 8,364 feet tall, it currently ranks at number thirty. Yet the blast that occurred at 8:31 a.m. on May 18, 1980, has made Mount St. Helens one of the most famous, most visited, and most climbed mountains in the world.

Perhaps it's because the volcano had been relatively quiet for 123 years before it blew. Or maybe it's because the eruption destroyed 220 homes, 17 miles of railroad, 150 square miles of land, 57,000 acres of timber, thousands of deer and elk, a couple hundred black bears, and millions of birds, fish, and other small animals.

Hours after the eruption, the water 40 miles downstream at Castle Rock was still hovering at 100°F. The ash that was blown up into the sky came down as far away as Montana and Denver, and it made the skies over Yakima so dark at 8:30 in the morning that the streetlights turned on.

Despite the fact that the area had been officially evacuated, fifty-seven people died as a result of the eruption, including a cranky, stubborn, eighty-four-year-old man named Harry Truman, who lived with his sixteen cats and a pink Cadillac just 5 miles from the mountain.

Truman had lived on the mountain for years, operating a rustic tourist lodge on the south shore of Spirit Lake. In the spring of 1980, when the volcano began rumbling and state officials started getting folks to leave the area, Truman refused to go. He softened a bit at the pleas to leave that were sent to him by a fifth-grade class in Michigan, but he stayed put anyway, telling a local reporter, "If this place is gonna go, I want to go with it, 'cause if I lost it, it would kill me in a week anyway." The mountain blew two months later, obliterating the lodge and burying Truman and his cats under tons of ash. Today, both a ridge overlooking the site and a trail are named in his memory.

The story of Harry Truman is told at the Hoffstadt Bluff Visitor Center, one of five visitor centers along Spirit Lake Memorial Highway (State Route 504) that tell about Mount St. Helens from a different perspective. For example, the Silver Lake Visitor Center offers the best view of the mountaintop (weather permitting), while the Coldwater Ridge Visitor Center focuses on the effects the blast had on the animals in the area.

To get to Spirit Lake Memorial Highway (State Route 504), head east from I-5 at exit 49. It will take you about two hours to get to the visitor centers from Seattle. For more information call (360) 247-3900 or visit www.fs.fed.us/gpnf/mshnvm.

APE CAVE

The 12,810-foot-long lava tube called Ape Cave, on the western slope of Mount St. Helens, is the longest unbroken lava tube cave in the United States and one of the longest such tubes in the world.

OK, but what's a lava tube cave?

Glad you asked! Lava tube caves are formed when flowing lava cools rapidly enough on the top and the bottom to solidify, while molten lava continues to flow inside. When the lava on the inside drains away, the outer lava crust is left in place.

Ape Cave was discovered by a logger named Lawrence Johnson, who was working in the woods in the late 1940s when he noticed a tree growing at an unusual angle. That led him to a sinkhole, which led him to a dark tunnel that seemed to have no end and to a cavern that seemed to have no bottom.

Johnson and his logging crew didn't have the tools, or the courage, to head for the unknown end of the cave, but a group of Boy Scouts and a cave-exploring dad did. The troop became the first group to explore the cave in detail; because they went by the moniker the Mount St. Helens Apes, the cave became known as Ape Cave. While that Boy Scout connection disappoints folks who head here thinking Ape Cave has something to do with the mythical Bigfoot creature said to roam the region, the cave offers plenty of geologic wonders.

Ape Cave, now extensively mapped, is open to the public. There's an interpretive center at the cave's entrance and an easily accessible lower cave with mudflow-covered floors and an impressive "lava ball" wedged into the ceiling. A more difficult to maneuver upper cave area has large rock piles and an 8-foot lava fall.

Ape Cave is near the town of Cougar, at the Mount St. Helens National Volcanic Monument. During the summer an interpretive naturalist leads tours through the lower part of the cave. For directions, hours, and more information, phone (360) 247-3900 or log on to www.fs.fed.us/gpnf/mshnvm.

Meet the Mighty Spud

Richland

Grouped together at the confluence of the Yakima, Snake, and Columbia Rivers are Kennewick, Richland, and Pasco, three cities so closely aligned that they're called the Tri-Cities. Although each city has its own personality, they share the geographic distinction of being near the massive Hanford Site, the former plutonium production facility that is now a huge toxic cleanup project. On the bright side, the farmland in this region sends plenty of potatoes, asparagus, apples, corn, and other agricultural products to market, most notably the world's second-largest crop of hops. The area is also becoming known for its wineries, breweries, and its annual July hydroplane race.

The Mighty Spud welcomes visitors to the Columbia River Exhibition of History, Science, and Technology.

The region's plutonium past is clearly the most curious thing about this area. You can't visit the decommissioned plutonium plants or (since September 11, 2001) the operating nuclear power plant, but you can stop at the Columbia River Exhibition of History, Science, and Technology (CREHST) in Richland. Exhibits detail the area's role in the Manhattan Project, and there's a slew of scale models of the early reactors and the waste tanks. The real fun, though, starts when you use the Geiger counter to check your personal level of radiation, try using the robotic manipulator to move "radioactive" objects around, and decide if you want to buy a pocketful of Atomic Marbles, which, you might be reassured to learn, are not at all radioactive, despite their greenish-brown tint.

CREHST isn't just about nukes, though. The agricultural exhibits feature an animated display hosted by an anthropomorphized potato called the Mighty Spud, while other exhibits chronicle the local discovery of woolly mammoth bones and, more recently, a 9,200-year-old skeleton dubbed Kennewick Man that is challenging long-held theories about the migratory patterns of early Eurasian peoples.

CREHST, located at 95 Lee Boulevard in Richland, is open daily. For information phone (509) 943-9000 or visit www.crehst.org.

Beer Blast
Richland

The Tri-Cities area is not only home to the world's first operating pluto-nium reactor, it's part of a significant hops-growing region. So what bet-ter way would there be to honor the local heritage than to open a brewpub that serves beers with nuclear names?

That's exactly what they do at the Atomic Ale Brewpub and Eatery in Richland, where the small-batch beers sport names such as Atomic Amber, Half-Life Hefeweisen, and Plutonium Porter. They further acknowledge the area's role in World War II defense work by hanging up historic photographs from the days when crews worked around the clock building the Hanford Engineer Works, and by giving their desserts explosive-sounding names such as Plutonium Porter Chocolate Con-tainment Cake and B-Reactor Brownies.

Although the Atomic Ale Brewpub and Eatery is a colorful place to visit today, the building site has an equally colorful past. During World War II the women's barracks for the Hanford Site were located right across the street. After the war an A&W Drive In restaurant sprouted here, complete with roller-skating servers. According to local legend, actress and Playboy playmate Sharon Tate, who was later killed during the infamous Manson Family murders in California, worked as one of those servers.

The Atomic Ale Brewpub and Eatery is located at 1015 Lee Boule-vard in Richland, right off of George Washington Way, which is the main street in town; phone (509) 946-5465.

EXPLOSIVE ADVERTISING

Richland's Atomic Ale Brewpub and Eatery isn't the only area business that gets a charge out of using "Atomic" in its name. You'll find the Atomic Auto Body shop and Atomic Records in Richland, Atomic Foods and Laundry in Pasco, and, in Kennewick, the Atomic Health Center and Atomic Screen Printing.

In Richland, the city that *Time* magazine declared to be "an atomic age utopia" in 1949, the local high school still calls all its sports teams "The Bombers"; the teams use an atomic mushroom cloud as their logo. The school adopted the moniker in honor of a specific B-17 bomber made by the Boeing Company in 1944. This particular bomber, *Day's Pay,* was so named because 51,000 Hanford workers each donated a day's pay to build the bomber as their contribution to the war effort. There is also a mural of B-17 bombers in formation on the side of the school gymnasium.

Giant Ginseng

Ridgefield

Ginseng is considered a magical forest root. It grows wild in areas of Japan and China and in some parts of the eastern United States. In the belief that ginseng offers everything from improved energy and vitality to relief from diabetes, obesity, impotence, and all manner of other ills, folks put ginseng in tea, slice it into recipes, and swallow it as a powder, in capsules, and in pills.

Unfortunately, wild ginseng is extremely expensive and, in the United States, categorized as an endangered plant. Despite the fact that many people believe

The world's largest ginseng root weighs 2.35 pounds and resides in a tank of vodka.

7 YEAR NORTH AMERICAN GINSENG
(Panax quinquefolium)
2.35 LBS (37 OZ)
GROWER: DON HOOGESTEGER 1997

farmed ginseng isn't as potent as the wild root, ginseng is becoming an ever more popular crop. Wisconsin farmers currently grow 85 percent of the nation's ginseng, but farmers in Washington and Oregon are discovering that the temperate Northwest climate is very conducive to growing this lucrative crop as well.

In fact, the Northwest soil and the long growing season are so well matched to growing ginseng that in 1988 the folks at Pacific Rim Ginseng in Ridgefield harvested what is considered to be the world's largest ginseng root. "The Big Root," as the current owners call it, weighs 2.35 pounds and has an arm spread measuring 28 inches. The root body is 16 inches tall, with a circumference of 8.5 inches. Before this root came along, the root believed to be the world's largest was in China; it weighed just 1.6 pounds.

The Big Root was grown by Don and Joy Hoogesteger, the original owners of Pacific Rim Ginseng and well known in the ginseng-growing community. To preserve the record-breaking root, they put it in an eleven-gallon fish tank and filled the tank with a well-known preserva-

SEEDS OF AN INDUSTRY

On April 6, 1926, a Swallow biplane left Pasco, Washington, on the maiden flight of Varney Air Lines. This launched the country's first contracted air mail service and the beginning of U.S. commercial air transportation. Varney Air Lines later grew into United Airlines.

tive: vodka. A few years later, when Darren and Kristin Deputy purchased the farm from the Hoogestegers, the vodka-infused ginseng root was part of the package. The root now sits on a table in the farm store, tipsy but regal.

You can visit the Big Root at the Pacific Rim Ginseng store in Ridgefield. To get there, take I-5 south to exit 9, turn left onto 179th Street, then turn left onto Tenth Avenue. The farm and the store are about a mile down the road on the left, at 20004 NW 10th Avenue. Phone (360) 887-3128 or log on to www.pacificrimginseng.com.

DON'T SHOOT THAT SASQUATCH

During the 1960s and 1970s, Skamania County was a hotbed of Bigfoot sightings. Sasquatch seekers flocked to the area in hopes of spying the tall, hairy, apelike creature for themselves. In fact, folks were so intent on getting some proof of the existence of the forest creature that in 1969, Skamania County commissioners passed an emergency ordinance making it a crime to shoot, slay, or otherwise hurt any Bigfoot in any way. The law, which is still on the books, categorizes the crime as a gross misdemeanor punishable by up to a year in the county jail and/or a $1,000 fine.

In 1984, despite the fact that no one had even scratched or, for that matter, even seen a Sasquatch, county commissioners went a step further and declared that the entire county would be designated as a Bigfoot refuge.

Who Hauls? U-Haul.
Ridgefield

Although Portland, Oregon, 20 miles to the south, claims to be the "retail" birthplace of U-Haul, the folks in Ridgefield, Washington, insist that their town is the no-question-about-it actual "Birthplace of U-Haul." Folks in this town are so confident of that claim to fame, in fact, that they've added the factoid to the "Welcome to Ridgefield" sign downtown on Pioneer Street.

A call to U-Haul headquarters solves the mystery. "The idea for U-Haul was hatched in Portland," says a company spokesperson, "but the first U-Haul trailers were actually made in Ridgefield."

Welcome
RIDGEFIELD
birthplace of U-HAUL
elevation 266   population 2147

U-Haul, I-Haul. We all haul in Ridgefield.

Here's how it happened: In the summer of 1945 L. S. "Sam" Shoen and his wife, Anna Mary Carty Shoen, tried to rent a small trailer to move their possessions from Los Angeles to Portland. No such rental service existed, so the pair stuffed what they could in their car. After they settled into their new home, they realized that others faced the same problem when moving, so they opened a small business renting out one-way, do-it-yourself moving equipment to others. At first they rented out trailers purchased from others. But when those, often secondhand, vehicles proved unreliable and the business began to falter, the couple moved in with family in Ridgefield, Washington, and began manufacturing their own trailers in a garage on the ranch. That worked, and by the end of 1949 it was possible to rent a trailer one way throughout most of the United States, and by 1955, throughout Canada. The rest is U-Haul history.

Say Your Prayers in Style
Stevenson

Don Brown once said he was blessed by pneumonia. As a young boy lying in a hospital bed, Brown first spied rosaries hanging from the habits of the Sisters of Mercy who were caring for him. That sparked a lifelong fascination with prayer beads, which resulted in a collection that tops 4,000 rosaries and is famous around the world.

Brown's collection first went on display in the early 1970s at the tiny county historical museum in Stevenson. Space was tight and funding nonexistent, so 500 birdcage hangers were pressed into service as an inspirational but unorthodox display device.

These days, the Don Brown rosary collection rests in specially made cases at Stevenson's elaborate Columbia Gorge Interpretive Center. The birdcages have been replaced by museum-quality rods, and the exhibit space features carved wooden arches and piped-in religious music.

Each rosary, though, is still labeled with a numbered jeweler's tag that corresponds to an entry in Don Brown's typed inventory catalog. From that catalog we learn that the rosaries are made out of everything from semiprecious jewels and seashells to bullets, Native American trading beads, and olive pits. Size-wise, the collection ranges from tiny finger rosaries stored in thimbles or acorns to the world's largest rosary, which is 16 feet long and made of Styrofoam balls.

The collection also includes a rosary that a nun in Alaska made with Ping-Pong balls, rosaries that belonged to Lawrence Welk and John F. Kennedy, an American flag made out of thirty-nine rosaries pinned to a board, and a rosary intended to be strapped to a steering wheel to aid the saying of prayers on the highway.

Don Brown didn't drive, but he died in a traffic accident in 1975, at the age of eighty. Although he was buried with the rosary he had in his pocket that day, museum officials suspect he would have preferred it if the rosary had been made part of the collection.

The Don Brown rosary collection is on display at the Columbia Gorge Interpretive Center, just off State Route 14 in Stevenson. For information call (800) 991-2338 or check the center's Web site, www.columbia gorge.org.

STATE MARRYING CAPITAL

According to the folks at the Skamania County Historical Society, Stevenson, the county seat, was once known as the "Marrying Capital" of the state. From the early 1900s through 1960, when most other towns were adopting waiting periods, eager brides and grooms could show up in Stevenson and purchase a license to get married that very same day.

There was just one slight wrinkle: The best-known justice of the peace was also the town barber. That meant that barbershop customers were often pressed into service as witnesses to a short-notice marriage ceremony, sometimes standing up for a couple midshave. It also meant that men who set out to get a haircut often returned home hours later, because they had to wait in line behind dozens of couples getting hitched by the barber.

Wolf at the Door

Tenino

That howling you hear coming from the woods just north of Tenino could be wolves. Or it might be people. Often it's both.

That's because Wolf Haven, which offers refuge to thirty or so captive-born gray wolves at a time, hosts regular Saturday night "Howl-ins"; visitors and wolves often end up spending the evening howling together.

"Unwanted" wolves find a home at Wolf Haven, where howling is encouraged.

Wolf Haven was created as a sanctuary for "unwanted" wolves that were no longer needed by researchers, had been mistreated by zoos, or perhaps were abandoned by families who had mistakenly thought a wolf might make a good pet. Because these wolves have lost their fear of people, they cannot be returned to the wild. Instead, they get to live alone, in pairs, or in packs in enclosures that mimic their natural habitat as closely as possible. Visitors can view some of the residents on guided walking tours of the facility, but a few of the animals, such as the rare Mexican wolves, are kept isolated because they're part of a captive breeding program that is reintroducing wolves in the Southwest.

The refuge, located on eighty acres of lush forest, is open from March through December. In the spring and summer Wolf Haven offers hourly guided walking tours, overnight camping experiences, and those weekend Howl-ins that are extremely popular with families. Don't worry if you can't make it to an official Howl-in. Visitors on daytime walking tours often come home with stories of hearing the wolves begin howling in tune to the whistle of a passing train.

Wolf Haven is at 3111 Offutt Lake Road, 7 miles southeast of I-5, just south of Olympia. For more information call (888) 722-9653 or check the refuge's Web site, www.wolfhaven.org.

Say Cheese!

Toledo

In 1919 dairy farmers around Toledo got together to create the Cowlitz Valley Cheese Association and, beginning in 1920, the cooperative began celebrating its success with coffee and free cheese sandwiches for everyone who came to Toledo during their annual celebration.

The building that housed Toledo's cheese factory still stands at the corner of Augustus Street and Third Street, although cheese-making operations closed down in the 1940s. But Toledo still celebrates its cheesy connections with a cheese festival each July. These days Cheese Days include a parade, a queen's court, a frog-jumping contest, a classic car and hot-rod show, cow plop bingo, and other activities, but true cheese fans will be happy to know that coffee and free cheese sandwiches are still on the menu and there's still a chance to meet and mingle with the "Big Cheese."

Toledo is located about 25 miles southeast of Chehalis and about 8 miles east of Winlock, home of the World's Largest Egg and the annual Egg Day festival, which includes free egg salad sandwiches for all. For more information about the Cheese Days festival held each July, contact the Lewis County Convention and Visitor Bureau at (800) 525-3323 or visit www. tourlewiscounty.com.

All Hopped Up

Toppenish

Although the Pacific Northwest has become famous for coffee, it's also famous for microbreweries and brewpubs. Perhaps that has something to do with the fact that the Pacific Northwest, especially Washington's Yakima Valley, is the largest hops-producing region in the United States and second only to Germany in hops production worldwide.

That industry's history is celebrated with displays of equipment, artifacts, and historic photos at the American Hop Museum in Toppenish, Washington. Volunteers from area hop-growing families and people from the hop industries spent years turning the old cement Hop Growers Supply building into a mural-adorned homage to *Humulus lupulus*, the perennial vine whose flowers are used for flavoring beer.

The region's hop history is celebrated at the American Hop Museum. Unfortunately, there's no hops here.

The murals, which follow the hop crop from planting through marketing of the finished product, tell just part of the story. Inside the museum you'll find antique hop presses, a horse-drawn hop duster, tools, scales, old picking baskets, balers, and examples of the stencils hop companies plaster on their hop bags and bales. Be sure to look in the yard for giant, rusting hop-picking machinery. On weekends keep your ears open for the steady stream of real-life hop workers who stop by to share memories of the days when the hop vines were trained to grow on poles 12 to 15 feet high (not on the low trellises used today), and when every hop farmer had his own hop storage house and kiln for curing a harvested crop.

Here's something to ponder as you wander around the exhibits: Beer has been a staple in the American diet since before anyone set foot on Plymouth Rock. According to an entry in the log book of the *Mayflower,* a tour guide claims, a major reason the Pilgrims landed at Plymouth Rock instead of their original destination (New Amsterdam) was that they were dangerously low on beer! The ship stopped to allow crew members to negotiate with local settlers for some suds. The rest, as they say, is hop history.

The American Hop Museum is located at 22 South B Street in Toppenish. From I-82, take exit 50 about 3 miles into Toppenish, and turn left on Asotin Avenue. Turn left again on Toppenish Avenue and continue one block to South B Street. For hours and more information call (509) 865-HOPS (4677) or visit www.americanhopmuseum.org.

Native Night-Night

Toppenish

Staying in a hotel or camping out in a tent is always fun, but what about spending the night in a tepee?

The Yakama Nation RV Park Resort, on the ancestral grounds of the 1.4-million-acre Yakama Nation Reservation, is one of those modern-day RV parks that offers access to all the comforts of a well-equipped community: swimming pool, hot tub, weight room, jogging and walking trails, basketball and volleyball courts, a gift shop, library, and theater.

You can set up your own tent or fold down the comforter in your motor home, but if you'd like to try something different, you can opt to spend the night in one of the park's fourteen authentic cone-shaped Ojibwa-style tepees and watch the sun

Tent camping is fun, but the Yakama Nation RV Park Resort lets travelers bed down in tepees.

set over "Pahto," or Mount Adams. Each tepee is 25 feet across, sleeps seven to ten adults, and has a fire pit and picnic table right outside, so you can bring your whole tribe along.

Right next door to the RV park, you'll find the Yakama Nation Cultural Center, which chronicles the history of the Yakama Indians in a 76-foot-high building designed to resemble the ancient Yakama winter lodge.

The Yakama Nation RV Park Resort is located on 280 Buster Road, 22 miles south of Yakima, on US 97. Look for the carved wooden bears at the entrance. For more information phone (800) 874-3087 or log on to www.yakamanation.com.

Watching Paint Dry

Toppenish

Each June, bleachers are set up in the streets of Toppenish and folks start showing up early to claim their seats. There's no parade to watch, no marathon making its way through town, and no famous person scheduled to show up waving his hat. Nope. The people filling the bleacher seats are here to watch paint dry.

The crowds don't assemble simply to watch a new coat of white paint getting splashed onto a wall. Things aren't *that* slow in Toppenish. The draw is Toppenish's annual Mural-in-a-Day project, an event that challenges a team of artists to transform boring blank walls into exciting full-size murals featuring scenes from the area's history.

The tradition started back in 1989, the same year Washington State celebrated its centennial year. That first mural, *Clearing the Land,* was completed by fifteen artists in eight hours. Now, more than thirty murals dot the town, depicting the Old West, railroading, rodeos, farming, aviation events, the Yakama Indian Nation, and various historical events.

You can walk around town and inspect the murals close-up, or ride around in a Conestoga wagon pulled by mules while a tour guide relates the history of each mural. Or you can grab a seat in the bleachers while the team of artists is at work, watch the newest mural unfold, and then see how long it takes the paint to dry.

Toppenish, the self-proclaimed "City of Murals," holds its Mural-in-a-Day event on the first Saturday in June. To get to Toppenish, drive 20 miles south of Yakima on US 97. For more information call (800) 863-6375 or check out www.toppenish.net.

In Toppenish, watching paint dry is a spectator sport.

WHAT WERE THOSE THINGS?

On June 24, 1947, Kenneth Arnold was flying his small plane from Chehalis, Washington, to his home in Idaho. Approaching Mount Rainier at about three o'clock in the afternoon, Arnold saw a bright light in the sky, then watched with surprise as nine shiny objects raced at high speed along the top of the Cascade Range.

Arnold shared the story of this unusual encounter with an Oregon newspaper and described to the reporter how he'd witnessed the mysterious, gleaming, metallic-looking objects flying in a most unusual manner and formation and behaving "like a saucer would if you skipped it across the water."

National news outlets picked up the story, and despite an "official" Air Force investigation that determined Arnold's encounter was nothing more than an unusual cloud formation, similar UFO sightings were soon popping up all over the country. These unidentified flying objects were now being referred to as "flying saucers," thanks to Kenneth Arnold, who reported several other out-of-this-world encounters before his death in 1984.

Vintage Baseball
Vancouver

For entertainment, soldiers stationed at the U.S. Army's Fort Vancouver around 1860 would play baseball. Their version of what is now America's most popular pastime was a bit different than the game as we know it today. For starters, they called it base ball (two words), and they played according to rules set forth by the National Association of Base Ball Players, which declared that:

- Ballists (as the players were called) had to play bare-handed. No gloves were allowed.
- The hurler (also known as the pitcher) had to pitch the ball underhand instead of overhand.
- A ball caught on the fly or the first bound (bounce) was considered an out.
- "Fair fouls," balls that touched fair territory before going out of the playing field, remained in play.
- No fielder was permitted to use his hat to catch the ball.

Think you could play by these rules or even follow the game? You get a chance to find out each summer when the folks from the Vancouver National Historic Reserve host one or more evenings of 1860s vintage base ball on the parade grounds of the Fort Vancouver National Historic Site. The teams are made up of "soldiers" from the first Oregon Volunteer Infantry and "base ballists" from the Vancouver Occidentals Base Ball Club, all dressed in period uniforms. If you go, you'll be called a crank, but don't be offended. That's what spectators were called back in the 1860s.

To help set the mood, pregame activities include a historical talk about base ball as a pastime for soldiers and civilians, and period music played by a brass band. Throughout the game an appropriately attired umpire explains the calls he's making and old-time cranks in vintage clothing mingle in the stands with us modern-day cranks.

The Fort Vancouver National Historic Site was the administrative headquarters and main supply depot for the Hudson's Bay Company's fur-trading operations in the Pacific Northwest. An archaeological site, it contains a museum and several reconstructed buildings.

To get there from I-5, take the Mill Plain exit and head east to Fort Vancouver Way. The Fort Vancouver Visitor Center is on Evergreen Boulevard. For more information about the site and the dates of the summer base ball games, call (800) 832-3599 or check the Web site at www.nps.gov/fova.

What's a strike?

It Just Keeps Going and Going and Going . . .

Vancouver

Long before we started bringing apples to our teachers or eating an apple a day to keep the doctor away, the fruit had been the stuff of legends. Adam and Eve were tempted by a shiny apple, and in Greek and Roman mythology, golden apples symbolize or reward love and beauty. Then there are the apple-related heroics associated with William Tell and Johnny Appleseed.

Old Apple Tree Park

Washington's oldest apple tree has its own park and its own annual celebration.

243

Washington, where the apple is the official state fruit, has one or two apple legends of its own. Tops among them is the location of the state's oldest fruit-bearing apple tree. While some claim the oldest apple tree must be somewhere in eastern Washington, the pomme producer that gets the official nod is located in a park in Vancouver, in the southwestern part of the state.

Apples, the story goes, first arrived in Washington in 1826, on a Hudson's Bay Company sailing ship. That next spring, seeds from a specially chosen "good luck" apple were planted at Fort Vancouver. Now Washington is the number one apple-growing state, producing more than twenty-five million boxes of apples each year. Good luck indeed.

The oldest apple tree in the Northwest is located in a park just north of Vancouver's waterfront Columbia Shores area. A great time to visit the tree is during the Old Apple Tree Celebration, usually held the first Saturday in October from 10:00 a.m. to 2:00 p.m. at the Old Apple Tree Park on Columbia Way, just east of the I-5 bridge in Vancouver. The festival celebrates the longevity of the tree and features Heritage Tree walks, historic tours, and scavenger hunts. Best of all, the Urban Forestry Commission gives away state-grown apples and cuttings from the Old Apple Tree. For more information call (360) 696-8031.

Very Egg-citing

Winlock

Founded in 1873, Winlock, in Lewis County, became the center of a thriving farming community. Chicken farms and hatcheries were scattered throughout the valley, and the town's location right near the railroad line facilitated the shipment of eggs and fresh-hatched chicks. In fact, by the early 1920s Lewis County was the second-largest egg producer in the United States, and during Winlock's busiest years, up to 2.5 million chicks were shipped out annually from the depot to spots around the country.

The world's largest egg gets a regular touch-up courtesy of the local high school art class.

Deservedly, Winlock became known as the Egg Capital of the World. So it was no surprise that when a parade was announced to celebrate the completion of a regional highway, Winlock entered a float featuring a wood-framed egg with white canvas stretched over it. The "world's largest egg," mounted on a Model T Ford, was such a big hit that the town made a more permanent giant egg out of tin and mounted it on a wooden platform with a lattice base.

Over the years the tin version has been replaced by giant eggs made from concrete, wire mesh, and, more recently, fiberglass. Although the town of Mentone, Indiana, tries to claim that *it* has the world's largest egg, Winlock residents refuse to crack under the pressure.

Don't think for a moment that the folks in Winlock take their egg for granted. Over the years artists from the local high school have painted and decorated the egg for Easter and other occasions, and recently, in a fit of patriotism, it was transformed into an egg-shaped American flag. Each year, during the third week in June, the town still celebrates Winlock Egg Days with a parade, a carnival, and free egg salad sandwiches for all.

To see the egg, take exit 63 from I-5 and head west to Winlock on State Route 505. Then just look around for the giant egg. For more information phone (360) 785-4494.

Apple-Shaped Golf Green
Yakima

Yakima is smack-dab in the middle of Washington apple country, so it's no surprise that just about everyone, including the owners of a local golf course, would get into the act of celebrating one of the area's top crops.

The Apple Tree Golf Course, on the outskirts of Yakima, is built on an old apple orchard. During harvest season you can still pick apples from the trees along the course, which has sixty sand bunkers, water hazards on eight holes, and a challenging signature hole in the shape of Yakima's favorite fruit. This hole, number 17, is a 170 yard par 3, requiring a tee shot over water to an apple-shaped island green. There's also a sand trap in the apple's leaf, and a bridge across the water forms the apple stem.

So, does a hole in one a day keep the doctor away?

The Apple Tree Golf Course is located on the west side of Yakima at 8804 Occidental Avenue. Phone (509) 966-5877 or log on to www.appletreegolf.com.

What would you take with you to an apple-shaped island? Your golf clubs, of course.

Teapot Dome Gas Station
Zillah

Travel between Yakima and Sunnyside along I-82 and you'll come upon a turnout for the town of Zillah and its 15-foot-tall teapot complete with sheet metal handle and concrete spout. No, it's not a mirage. It's a classic bit of roadside architecture that's been providing travelers both a needed service and a history lesson since the early 1920s.

Built in 1922, the Teapot Dome Gas Station was the oldest functioning gas station in the United States for many years. It still is the cutest—working or not.

SOUTH AND SOUTHWEST

Jack Ainsworth thought up this structure in 1922, after a night of drinking moonshine and playing cards. Ainsworth and his buddies were appalled by the outcome of President Warren G. Harding's decision a year earlier to transfer the control of naval oil reserves at Teapot Dome, Wyoming, and Elk Hills, California, from the navy to the Department of the Interior. It seems that Secretary of the Interior Albert Fall had leased those oil fields to two businessmen who had given him what ultimately were deemed to be illegal "loans." Investigations ensued, fines were paid, folks ended up in jail, and the oil fields reverted to government control in 1927.

Ainsworth built the Teapot Dome Gas Station to poke fun at the whole situation while the trials were under way, and until it ceased commercial operation in 2003, it was the oldest functioning gas station in the United States. Zillah officials are now raising funds to purchase the teapot, which is on the National Register of Historic Places, and relocate it in town, where it might serve as a welcome kiosk for visitors.

For now, the Teapot Dome Gas Station is located at 14691 Yakima Valley Highway, 15 miles southeast of Yakima. From I-82, take exit 54 and cross over the freeway. The teapot is on the southwest side of the road.

EASTERN WASHINGTON

CANADA

Okanogan
National
Forest

Colville
National
Forest

97

Conconully
20 Republic
25

97
Omak
20

Kettle
Falls
20

153
21

395
20

Columbia River Grand
Coulee
Dam

97A
97
Grand Coulee
25 231 395 Elk

209
172
17

2
2
Davenport Spokane
90

28
2

97A 2
Soap Lake
28
21
28 231

28
Soap Lake
195 27

97
George 283
Moses Lake
271

90 Moses Lake
90 Lind 395
Colfax 272

243 24
17
26 26 26
Pullman 27

82 240
260
21
127 195

241 22
395 124
Dayton 12
Uniontown 12
Clarkston
Asotin

221 82
Walla Walla
12
Umatilla
National
Forest
129

14

OREGON

IDAHO

0   50 Miles

0   50 KM

EASTERN WASHINGTON

While western Washington is wet and mild, the territory east of the Cascade Mountains is decidedly drier and experiences more extreme swings in temperature. That's not the only thing that separates east from west. Folks in the east pride themselves on being tougher and more self-sufficient than those "latte lovers" in the west. Over the years there have even been campaigns advocating that the eastern part of the state secede from the west.

I hope they stay connected. That way we can continue to celebrate the fact that Washington has an annual outhouse race, a gala Lentil Festival, a town that chooses an official grouch each year, and a museum dedicated to robots.

Branded

Asotin

Located in the far southeastern corner of the state, at the confluence of the Snake River and Asotin Creek, Asotin serves as a jumping-off point for recreation activities in the Hells Canyon area. It's also the home of the Asotin County Fair, which was the first yearly county fair in the state and is the place to go to see one of the nation's largest collections of branding irons.

The tradition of using the white-hot burning end of an iron or steel tool to leave a special identifying mark on an animal's hide reaches back 4,000 years to the Egyptians. The custom spread throughout the American West along with the rise of cattle ranching that set herds of cattle out to graze on the open range. Early branding irons bore a rancher's initial, or perhaps a number or a simple design. Over time the designs became more intricate, and brand books were developed to keep track of who owned what brand.

More than 200 branding irons, along with a wide variety of brand books and other tools of the trade, ended up in the hands of the late Asotin-area rancher Bob Weatherly. He just couldn't bear the fact that branding irons from old homesteads in his area were being sold to city folk as quaint antiques, so he began buying up every brand he could. He expanded the collection to include irons from throughout the West, and eventually donated his large collection of branding irons to the Asotin Museum, which displays them all on a wall in the museum's vintage pole barn.

The museum itself is housed in a building that once served as the town's funeral home; the previous owners left behind a casket that is now part of a historical display. Out behind the museum you'll find a collection of other area buildings that were dismantled and rebuilt on-site, including a ca. 1881 square-nailed cottage from Theon, which became a ghost town when the local water supply dried up.

The Asotin Museum, at 215 Filmore Street in Asotin (at Third), is open from March through October. For more information phone (509) 243-4659.

Postal Persistence

Clarkston

Hells Canyon, North America's deepest river gorge, stretches from Hells Canyon Dam northward for 75 miles to the Washington-Oregon border. The canyon is part of the Hells Canyon National Recreation Area, which includes wilderness that is at once spectacularly inviting and excessively rugged. For example, the Seven Devils mountain range tops out at 9,000 feet (at He Devil Mountain) and then drops 1.5 miles to the mouth of Granite Creek. Pretty much the only way to get around the area is by river raft or jet boat.

Since the early 1900s the challenging terrain hasn't stopped the U.S. mail from getting through. In fact, ever since 1919, when the U.S. Postal Service awarded its very first river route mail contract, the hardy year-round residents of Hells Canyon have been getting weekly mail delivery via boat. True, it only shows up once a week, but then again, these mail carriers have had to deal with high water in addition to the traditional snow, rain, heat, and gloom of night.

In the 1940s a resourceful fellow named Kyle McGrady was delivering mail and supplies to about 350 people along a 99-mile route. He'd take homing pigeons along for the ride so he could send messages home to his wife, Florence. Sometimes those messages included a list of groceries the Hells Canyon residents wanted Florence to gather up for them, but one special message that Florence kept around for years simply said, "Happy Birthday."

Today the handful of ranchers who live in Hells Canyon still get their mail delivered by boat. The mail boat is now a jet boat tour that leaves each Wednesday from Clarkston. It takes passengers 70 miles upriver for an overnight trip that includes a tour of the canyon, a night's stay at a cozy lodge, and a chance to help deliver the mail.

For information about Hells Canyon and the range of available raft and river tours, call the Hells Canyon Visitor Association at (877) 774-7248 or visit www.hellscanyonvisitor.com.

Football Match Memorialized
Colfax

The folks in Colfax either have an insatiable desire for revenge or a great sense of humor. Visit the town's Codger Pole and you'll understand it's both.

The 65-foot-tall sculpture is the largest chain-saw sculpture in the world, and it commemorates the infamous 1988 replaying of a football game that the Colfax Bulldogs lost to the St. John Eagles on a snowy November day back in 1938. The score: 14 to 0. Ouch.

Most communities would have put that game and its painful memories behind them as quickly as possible. Not the citizens of Colfax. For years that loss stuck in the craw of players and fans alike. After fifty years, some local sports fans decided that enough was enough. A rematch was called. The original players, cheerleaders, and schoolmates, all now fifty years older, were invited to come back to town to try again.

The challenge was accepted, and the Codger Bowl, as it became known, was scheduled for September 1988. Everyone, it seems, got into the act of reliving the past: cheerleaders and marching bands squeezed back into uniform; fans attended the pep rally, the bonfire, the parade, and the pregame dance.

Not everything was the same though. On game day, instead of playing tackle football, the old codgers played tag football. Instead of helmets, the players wore commemorative caps. The outcome? This time the Colfax Bulldogs won with a score of 6 to 0.

Codger Pole honors the Codger Bowl, a "do-over" football match that took fifty years to schedule.

To commemorate that long-awaited win, the town commissioned well-known sculptor Jonathan LaBenne (a.k.a. Jonathan the Bear Man) to create a suitable monument. He bundled up five red cedar logs into one fat pole and then carved the helmeted faces of fifty-two Colfax Bulldogs on it. At the top, he placed a 15-foot-tall ponderosa pine player, complete with helmet, football, and vintage uniform.

The chain-saw sculpture now stands in a park on Main Street in Colfax. A carved plaque at the bottom of the pole celebrates the fact that the rematch "gave us guys a chance to fulfill that dream that every seventy-year-old kid hangs on to: Playing one more game . . . "

To see the Codger Pole, head north on U.S. Highway 195 from Pullman to Colfax. The pole is at John Crawford Boulevard on Main Street.

Watch Out for That Outhouse
Conconully

The population in Conconully peaked at about 500 back in 1888, when the town became the Okanogan county seat. That honor lasted only until 1915, when the town of Okanogan took over that role.

Conconully now has a population of fewer than 200. Over the years it's suffered plenty of other indignities: Fire destroyed many of the town's buildings in 1892, and in 1894 a flood swept away most of what had been rebuilt. Forest fires, mining closures, and other disasters have hit the town as well.

No wonder, then, that when someone suggested the town host a mid-January Outhouse Race, no one blinked an eye. That was about twenty years ago, and it turns out outhouse racing is now Conconully's most well-attended annual event. Each year, more than one hundred contestants show up from near and far to race about a dozen homemade outhouses down a gently sloping one-block course.

There are, of course, some rules for what constitutes a race-ready outhouse. Each nonmotorized, nonsteering privy entered in the race must:

- be made out of wood or wood by-products,
- be mounted on two skis (no metal or steel skis allowed, but fiber-glass and plastic are fine),
- have three sides and a full roof,

Funky one-seater outhouses of all shapes and sizes race through the streets of Conconully each January as part of the annual Outhouse Race.

• be at least 5 feet tall and 2½ feet square, and

• be equipped with a toilet seat, toilet paper hanger, and toilet paper.

Winning racers receive cash awards and trophies made by local craftspeople; each trophy resembles a miniature outhouse.

Can't wait to go? The Outhouse Race is held each year on the third Saturday in January. Conconully is located about 20 miles northwest of the towns of Omak and Okanogan. For more information phone (877) 826-9050 or visit www.conconully.com.

Wild West Desperado
Davenport

Who needs made-up Westerns when the stories of real outlaws are so darned good? Take the story of Harry Tracy, a Wisconsin boy turned bad. Very bad. Bad to the bone.

Tracy allegedly spent some time with the notorious Hole in the Wall Gang, but in 1899 he hooked up with David Merrill to pull off a string of robberies and holdups in Portland, Oregon. The pair became known as the Black Mackinaw Bandits because they always wore long black raincoats while "on the job."

Both men spent some time in the Oregon State Penitentiary for these crimes, but succeeded in breaking out in early June 1902, killing several guards on their way out of the building. They headed north to Seattle, where Tracy killed Merrill and a few policemen before heading to the eastern part of the state and boldly eluding capture.

That is, until early August, when Tracy landed at the Eddy Ranch near Creston, in eastern Washington's wheat country. After hanging out and relaxing on the ranch for a few days, Tracy was visited by a five-man posse. These sharpshooting townsfolk succeeded in shooting Tracy twice in the leg before he found cover in a wheat field. Not wanting to wade through the wheat and risk getting shot at by Tracy, the posse surrounded the field and waited until morning. But in true outlaw fashion, Tracy had vowed that he'd never be taken alive. So while he lay wounded in the field, he shot himself in the head.

The grisly story of desperado Harry Tracy was detailed in newspapers throughout the Northwest and later became the subject of dime novels, plays, nonfiction books, and a few movies. These days, you can also learn the story of Harry Tracy at the Lincoln County Historical Museum in Davenport. There they display his plaster death mask, a frying pan he used while on the run, a bullet from his cartridge belt, and lots of gruesome photos.

The Lincoln County Historical Museum is located on Seventh and Park Streets in Davenport, 35 miles west of Spokane on U.S. Highway 2. The museum, which also displays more sedate exhibits about the history and culture of the area, is open from May through September. For hours and more information call (509) 725-6711 or visit www.davenport wa.org/historical_society.htm.

Landlord Tree
Dayton

A tree known locally as the "Lone Pine of Eckler Mountain" (actually it's a Douglas fir) was once listed in *Ripley's Believe It or Not* as "the only tree in the U.S.A. which owns the land it stands on."

Turns out there's a "replacement" tree in Georgia that also seems to own its own land, but Dayton's Lone Pine is the very same tree detailed in the property deed filed at the Columbia County Court House on December 15, 1922.

On that day, John and Dollie Gantz declared the "Cahill Fir Tree" to be a public monument and a landmark forever dedicated to the memory of William and Angeline Cahill, who planted the original sapling on their homestead in 1878.

To make sure that the tree would remain unmolested, the Gantz family added a surrounding plot of land 30 feet in diameter and stipulated that the land and the tree were to be forever off-limits to farming or "interference" of any kind, either by "digging the roots or mutilating the body in any manner except that the limbs of said tree may be properly trimmed up 12 feet from the ground."

The deed has been honored all these years, and today the Cahill Fir Tree stands apart from other trees at the junction of Crall Hollow Road and Eckler Mountain Road in Dayton (on U.S. Highway 12), a good spot to look out at Mount Adams, Mount Rainier, and Mount St. Helens.

Since 1922 this tree has been the sole "owner" of the land under and around it. Trespassing allowed.

It Ain't Easy Being Green
Dayton

According to the Washington State Asparagus Commission, Washington produces about eighty million pounds of asparagus each year, or about 40 percent of all the asparagus grown in the United States.

What happens to all those tender green shoots? Some end up in restaurants and at groceries, but most of them get canned under the Green Giant label at the world's largest asparagus cannery, which is conveniently located right here in Dayton. Cannery workers pack about 3 million cases or thirty-six million cans of asparagus each year.

Area asparagus farmers and cannery workers are a loyal and, it seems, lighthearted bunch. During the 1970s and 1980s, one local farmer would outline and heavily fertilize a spot on his hillside in the shape of the Jolly Green Giant. As the season progressed, the figure would get greener and easier to make out. Unfortunately, though, rains would often distort or wash away important parts of the big green man.

This big guy keeps watch over Dayton.

In 1991 a group of local residents tried a different approach. The new Jolly Green Giant is still on a hillside, but now he's 300 feet tall, 40 feet wide, and outlined with patio blocks that should stay put.

Although the image is flat, it's still awfully charming to round the bend near Dayton and be greeted by the Jolly Green Giant. To see him for yourself, head west of Dayton on US 12 for about a mile. While you're in town, be sure to pick up a walking-tour brochure and poke around a bit. Dayton has 117 buildings listed on the National Register of Historic Places, including the Columbia County Courthouse, the oldest courthouse in the state.

For more information call (800) 882-6299 or visit www.historic dayton.com

Robot Hut

Elk

When John Rigg was a kid, he got a really cool robot as a Christmas present. Rigg grew up and became a successful electronics and audio engineer in Seattle, but the fascination with robots never left him, so he started collecting robots, making robots, swapping robots with other robot fans, and dreaming of a place where he could display his growing robot collection.

In Elk, about a half-hour drive from Spokane, Rigg found a small ranch and built something he calls the Robot Hut. It's not a hut at all, but actually a huge barn-size building filled with shelf after shelf of robots. More than 2,500 of them. There's even a giant 20-foot-tall robot affixed to the outside that spouts steam at unsuspecting visitors.

Inside, it's a robot fan's paradise. Everywhere you look there are robots either made or collected by John Rigg. Those square-headed Rock'em, Sock'em Robots are here, along with Rosie from *The Jetsons,* the see-through Mr. Machine robot from the 1960s, and Atomic Robot Man toys from 1940s Japan.

Maria from the movie *Metropolis* has a place of honor in the Robot Hut, as does Gort from *The Day the Earth Stood Still.* There's also plenty of space for various versions of Robby the Robot from the movie *Forbidden Planet,* the team of R2-D2 and C-3PO from *Star Wars,* B-9, the robot featured in the TV series *Lost in Space,* and a tall metal robot Rigg made using parts he had around the house, including an air filter, a motorcycle gas tank, and worn-out Dustbusters. The face on the Rigg robot is a rubber cast of Rigg's own face, and its eyes move back and forth. "My wife asked me to take that one out of the house," admits Rigg.

This cheery fellow is just one of the 2,500 robots that live in John Rigg's Robot Hut.

Rigg loves and knows the story behind every single robot in his collection, but he's partial to the ones he made himself, such as the Machine Man Band that took more than four months to complete. Reminiscent of the calliope band-in-a-box machines you'd come across in old-time circuses and sideshows, Rigg's Machine Man Band has forty-eight handmade pipes, several drums, and a variety of other noisemaking objects, all controlled by a computer program. The Machine Man Band loves to play tunes for visitors, but we warn you: It's loud!

The Robot Hut is open to visitors by appointment only. For more information e-mail John Rigg at robothut@yahoo.com or check his Web site, www.robothut.robotnut.com.

Pie for Everyone
George

Appropriately enough, the town of George, Washington, was dedicated on July 4, 1957. As part of the festivities, a half-ton cherry pie was assembled and baked in a huge Dutch brick oven. It took three hours to bake and another four hours to cool.

Ever since then, the town of George has celebrated the Fourth of July with a parade, a flag celebration, music, games, and a gala fireworks display. Each year the townsfolk also bake another giant cherry pie. They use the same 8-foot-square, 5-inch-deep pan that was used back in 1957, only now the pie weighs in at 1,500 pounds and uses more than 100 gallons of pie cherries, 200 pounds of sugar, 1½ cups of red food coloring, and a great deal of cutout pastry toppings.

Year after year, that qualifies this tasty pastry as the world's largest cherry pie. And year after year, thousands show up to help eat that pie.

And that's no lie.

George Washington never slept here. But every Fourth of July the folks in George, Washington, bake up a giant cherry pie in his honor.

The town of George, Washington, is midway between Ellensburg and Moses Lake at exit 149 on Interstate 90. For more information check the city's Web site at www.ci.george.wa.us.

A TOWN NAMED GEORGE

Some Western towns grew up around gold claims. Great location, access to water, or the coming of the railroad gave birth to other fine burgs. According to folks who were there, the creation of the town of George, Washington, was simply the result of a chance meeting of three men in a drugstore.

Sometime in the mid-1950s, the Bureau of Reclamation invited bids for the establishment of a town in the middle of a large unpopulated area of Grant County. Three businessmen who chanced to meet up in a pharmacy in the nearby town of Quincy got to talking and decided to put in a group bid. By the time the bid was awarded, however, only one man, Charlie Brown, still lived in the area. He bought the property, started planning his town, and realized that in a state named after the nation's first president he could go one step up the honorific chain by naming his town George.

They take the George Washington theme very, very seriously here. Every President's Day weekend, the town holds a birthday party for George Washington. Many businesses, such as the Martha Inn Cafe, sport George Washington–related names and decor year-round. The George thing even extends to the streets, which bear the names of different varieties of cherry trees. The town's main street is Montmorency, which, legend has it, was the type of cherry tree young George Washington chopped down. Other streets bearing cherry tree names include Royal Anne, Richmond, Van, Nanking, Naden, Deacon, and Windsor Avenues, and, of course, Bing Avenue.

Irrigation Illumination
George

A few years back, Scott and Janet Libbert figured out that if they turned their farm's 15-foot-tall irrigation sprinkler toward the highway, they could tap into the machinery's electrical wiring and use it to power the huge animated Christmas display that Scott had designed using rebar and spray-painted strings of lights.

Motorists driving by an otherwise bleak stretch of I-90 liked the Libberts' holiday lights so much that other farmers in the area decided they'd also turn their irrigation sprinklers toward the road and get Scott to design animated displays for their fields.

Libbert was happy to oblige, spending hours creating an animated scuba-diving Santa for one neighbor, a present-filled train with turning wheels and puffs of smoke for another, a jack-in-the-box that repeatedly popped up out of its box, and a jolly golfing Santa heading for the golf course.

Now, animated lighted displays powered by irrigation sprinklers are a community-wide holiday tradition. More than two dozen farmers use their sprinklers to light up more than twenty displays along the highway.

To see the Quincy Valley Christmas lights, drive along I-90 from George toward Moses Lake. Lighted displays also fill the fields on State Route 281, going north toward Quincy.

SO THAT'S WHERE WHEAT COMES FROM

Now that they have those little spritzers that gently mist the carrots, cabbage, and kale in the grocery store, can you really blame an urban dweller for being lulled into thinking that the greens are actually grown right there in the produce aisle?

"Wise up!" say the farmers in central Washington's Grant County. "That corn, them apples, and those there potatoes you're toting home from the grocery come from our fields, the ones you zip by at 70 mph on the interstate."

These days, you need only look out your car window to get the message. A group of farmers near the towns of George, Quincy, Ephrata, and Moses Lake, with fields along 30 miles of highway, now post identification signs out in front of their crops. That way, they figure, people who don't know the difference between a beanpole and a cornstalk can just read the signs to find out what's going on in the fields.

For those who don't bother to read the signs that announce CORN or POTATOES in progress, there's a 12-foot-tall, 40-foot-wide state-of-the-art electronic billboard strategically located on I-90 near George, at exit 149. The sign flashes agriculturally oriented messages such as CORN MAKES DIAPERS, BEEF MAKES COATING FOR FILM, and CRAYONS, TEXTBOOKS, PENCILS, AND PAPER ARE PRODUCTS OF AGRICULTURE at the folks in the 25,000 or so cars that pass by daily. Sprinkled in among the facts are a few farm jokes, such as "A pig's least favorite sport? Football."

Still don't get the message? Signs along the highway urge motorists to tune their radios to 1610 AM. The low-powered radio transmitter on the top of the giant sign broadcasts a continuous loop of chatty information for kids and adults about local crops, area farmers, food prices, food safety, and all sorts of other fascinating agriculture information.

If you feel you've had enough farm fodder, just keep driving. The radio signal only reaches for 10 or 12 miles.

CAN YOU YAHOO?

When Wylie Gustafson was growing up in northwestern Montana, his dad, a rancher and veterinarian, would entertain the family by playing guitar, singing cowboy songs, and yodeling.

Young Wylie grew up to be an accomplished singer, yodeler, and rancher himself, and now lives on a 120-acre horse and cattle ranch about 2 miles from the tiny town of Dusty (population eleven) with his wife, Kim, some buffalo, and a herd of quarter horses that his family breeds, trains, and sells.

When he's not at work on the ranch, Gustafson might be found showing off his winning roping and cutting skills at a rodeo or, more likely, out on the road with his band, Wylie and the Wild West, singing songs with titles like "Big Sky Lullaby" and "Montana Moon." The band tours the United States and abroad, playing an infectious strain of Western music laced with Gustafson's signature yodeling. And although the tall, lean, and fresh-faced band leader is a well-respected cowboy singer and songwriter with a growing following, it's his yodeling abilities that have gained him the most notice and notoriety. And the biggest headaches.

Back in 1996, known now as the ancient days of the Internet, an audio production company hired Gustafson to create and record a special yodel for Yahoo!, the Web search engine, to use in its very first television commercial. That unique yodel was then used in Yahoo!'s other commercials, which aired on everything from the Super Bowl to the Academy Awards. The yodel could also be heard on sound tracks, radio commercials, and the Internet. In fact, Gustafson's yodel became somewhat synonymous with Yahoo! and became the company's unofficial trademark.

You may not know his name or have heard his music, but you've probably heard him yodel.

There was one problem, though: Gustafson had only given his permission for the yodel to be used on that first commercial. For three years Gustafson tried to resolve the issue politely, which is, after all, the cowboy way. Unfortunately, he got no response from Yahoo! representatives. Gustafson finally took the issue to court, and a settlement was quickly arranged.

Now that's something we can all Yahoo! about.

To find out more about the music and touring schedule of Wylie Gustafson's band, Wylie and the Wild West, see their Web site, www.wylieww.com.

Wind-Powered Wonders
Grand Coulee

If you're planning to visit the man-made hydroelectric-power-producing marvel known as the Grand Coulee Dam, be sure to stop at Bicentennial Park in the town of Grand Coulee to gaze in delight at the wonderful wind-powered folk art garden created by Emil Gehrke.

Gehrke was an ironworker from Nebraska who lived with his wife in Grand Coulee for more than twenty years. Together they'd drive the countryside collecting all manner of castoff materials for Emil to use in his fanciful windmills. Anything could—and seemingly did—catch his fancy: cookie tins, plastic bowling pins, hubcaps, bicycle wheels, coffeepots, and bits and pieces of old farm machinery. Once back home, Emil would wire up the windmills and then his wife would paint them.

When Gerhke was alive, he displayed his windmills in his yard. Now that he's gone, many of his cast-away creations are displayed in a fenced-in public area along the highway, where volunteers from the community plant flowers and keep things tidy. No one has calculated the energy that might have been harvested from these windmills over the years, but it's a sure bet the brightly colored whirling wonders have generated thousands of hours of entertainment.

Gehrke's windmills are located in the North Dam Rest Area on State Route 155, between Grand Coulee and Electric City.

More Fun Than a Walk around the Equator

Grand Coulee Dam

No visit to the eastern part of Washington is complete without a stop at the Grand Coulee Dam.

Built in an around-the-clock effort between 1933 and 1942, the structure is grand indeed. It holds the title of the largest concrete dam in North America, stands twice as high as Niagara Falls, and is just a smidge less than a mile long. The dam is the third-largest producer of electricity in the world and the largest producer of hydroelectric power in the United States.

But wait! There's more: Grand Coulee Dam contains almost 12 million cubic yards of concrete. That's just enough cement, according to the handy Bureau of Land Reclamation guide distributed to visitors on-site, to build a 4-foot-wide, 4-inch-thick sidewalk 50,000 miles long, long enough to go around the equator twice.

But why go twice around the equator when you can spend a day touring the dam and learning about the incredible lengths thousands of Depression-era workers went to in order to complete the project?

Visitors to the Grand Coulee Dam can take a guided tour, witness an elaborate summertime laser light show, and watch impressive films about the Columbia River and the Grand Coulee, the spectacular gorge created by glaciers during the ice ages. The most entertaining and (don't tell the kids) educational part of any visit is the ride on the incline elevator that descends to the dam's third power plant, which was added to the facility in the 1970s. The fifty-passenger glass-fronted elevator travels 465 feet on a 45-degree incline, offering a spectacular view.

On your ride, try not to think too much about the seventy-seven workers who lost their lives in the construction of the dam (contrary to legend, no bodies are buried in the dam's concrete walls).

Start your visit to the Grand Coulee Dam at the Visitor Arrival Center, just north of the dam on State Route 155. In addition to touring the dam itself, you can pick up a flyer that will lead you on a walking tour of historic Coulee Dam, one of the small towns near the Grand Coulee Dam. Highlights of that tour include a stop at what the town claims is the "world's largest sandbox," a 12-million-cubic-yard pile of sand left over from the production of concrete during the construction of the dam.

For visiting hours and more information about the Grand Coulee Dam, call (509) 633-9265 or (800) 268-5332 or check out www.grand couleedam.org.

Town Grouch
Kettle Falls

Everyone wakes up on the wrong side of the bed once in a while and spends the morning frowning and feeling a wee bit cranky. It even happens to residents of Kettle Falls, a small town just 30 miles from the Canadian border and right next to Lake Roosevelt, the largest lake in the state.

A sign on the edge of town welcomes visitors to the area and lists the population as 1550 FRIENDLY PEOPLE AND ONE GROUCH. How can they be so sure about that grouch part? Well, anyone who walks around Kettle Falls once too often without a smile or a good word runs the risk of being elected the official Town Grouch.

As you might imagine, it's not an office that generates much campaigning. At least not by the nominees themselves. Usually other folks nominate people they think have been particularly grumpy, then they work hard to sell votes.

Sell votes? Isn't that illegal? Not here. Each grouch ballot costs 25 cents; the money from an annual average of 4,500 votes goes to worthy local causes. So in Kettle Falls, stuffing the ballot on behalf of a particularly cantankerous candidate is highly encouraged.

Votes are cast from April 1 through the last day of the Kettle Falls Town and Country Day celebration on the first weekend in June. Town and Country festivities include a "Grumpy Grouch Fun Run," a parade in which Town Grouch candidates ride in a faux jail cell, and a final session of frenzied campaigning and ballot stuffing. The winner keeps the title for a full year.

Kettle Falls is located on U.S. Highway 395, just west of Colville. For more information about Kettle Falls, call the Kettle Falls Chamber of Commerce at (509) 738-2300 or check the chamber's Web site, www .kettlefalls.com.

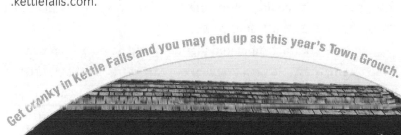

Get cranky in Kettle Falls and you may end up as this year's Town Grouch.

WASHINGTON STATE'S FOLK SONG

In 1941 the Bonneville Power Administration (BPA) was building a series of somewhat controversial dams on the Columbia River, which borders Washington and Oregon. The agency, which hoped to make a promotional movie about the project, gave a down-on-his-luck singer who'd been hanging around Portland, Oregon, a one-month stint on the project.

That singer turned out to be noted folksinger Woody Guthrie, but the troubadour's official one-month title was not singer or writer, but "information consultant." His assignment? To bang out as many songs as he could praising the dams, the work of the BPA, and the general concept of public power.

Guthrie's contract stipulated that he would be paid $266.66 to write a song a day. He didn't quite meet that mark, but he got surprisingly close. Guthrie penned twenty-six songs in thirty days, including "Jackhammer Blues," "Pastures of Plenty," "Hard Travelin'," and a song that called the Grand Coulee Dam, "just about the biggest thing that man has ever done."

One of the other songs he completed during his tenure as information consultant, "Roll on, Columbia," was adopted as Washington State's official folk song in 1987.

Start Your Threshers

Lind

Nestled deep in the heart of wheat-farming territory, the town of Lind has gained notoriety of sorts for an unusual annual event featuring combines, those huge 10,000-pound power-operated machines that farmers usually use to cut, thresh, and clean grain. In this competition, though, the goal of each combine driver is to make sure his or her rig can thrash the heck out of all oncoming farm machinery. The resulting metal-on-metal melee is accompanied by a lot of screaming and yelling from the drivers, from their "pit crews," and from the revved-up fans in the stands who can't wait to see which hopped-up combine will be left running after the dust settles.

The rules for entering the Combine Demolition Derby, as it's officially known, are pretty straightforward: Combines entered into competition must be at least twenty-five years old and deemed useless in the wheat

In Lind old combines don't rust away, they get entered in the Combine Demolition Derby.

field. The machinery can be modified, but all potentially dangerous reels, sickle guards, and glass must be removed. Fair enough.

That still leaves several tons of heavy metal and machinery with which to accomplish the mission of disabling and demolishing an opponent's combine to the point where it can no longer move. Two combines at a time are sent into battle; after each heat, a pit crew gets a short amount of time to try to repair a disabled rig so it can get back in the competition for a shot at the raucous, rattling "championship" round.

Beyond the sheer fun of giving a huge piece of rusting machinery one last hurrah, drivers are competing for serious prize money that tops out at $1,000 for the three combines still running at the end of the day and for the three machines deemed best decorated for battle.

The Combine Demolition Derby is held in Lind each year on the second weekend in June at the Lion's Club arena. Lind is located on U.S. Highway 395, southwest of the town of Ritzville. For more information visit the Lind Web site at www.lindwa.com.

Spotlight on Spuds

Moses Lake

Washington State produces about 20 percent of all U.S. potatoes. Most of these potatoes are grown in the eastern part of the state, in and around the Columbia Basin, where the climatic conditions, rich volcanic soil, abundant water, and long growing season make it possible to produce the world's highest yield per acre of potatoes.

So it's no surprise that the folks around here are pretty proud of their potato-producing prowess. In fact, potatoes are such an important part of life out here that for many years the Moses Lake Museum and Art Center hosted an art show on the theme of Baked, Mashed, or Fried.

The rules were simple: Potatoes could be the subject or the medium and the artwork could be inspired by people, places, or things associated with the potato industry.

The result? Over the years, the starchy staple most of us view simply as a vehicle for butter or sour cream inspired plenty of serious and not-so-serious artwork, everything from potato-shaped teapots to an engraving depicting a farmyard engagement party for a Russet and Little Red.

These days, artists are invited to submit work with either a potato or non-potato theme, but everyone who attends the museum's annual Gourmet Potato Luncheon is served the same thing: freshly baked potatoes with a choice of traditional and nontraditional toppings.

The Moses Lake Museum and Art Center, located at 228 West Third Avenue in Moses Lake, holds it annual Gourmet Potato Luncheon each February. For more information contact the museum at (509) 766-9395 or visit www.mlrec.com/museum.html.

Stampede and Suicide Race
Omak

Omak is the largest city in rural Okanogan County. They grow a lot of apples here and much of the delicate baby's breath sprigs that florists use to fill out birthday and anniversary bouquets. Omak's greatest claim to fame, however, is the annual Stampede and Suicide Race.

The stampede mixes a professional rodeo with a Wild West show, a carnival, and a Western art show, but it's the rough-and-tumble Suicide Race that creates the most excitement and, more recently, the most controversy.

See if you can figure out why:

The race starts with twenty riders who take off on a running start so that they can send their horses down an extremely steep slope called, eerily, Suicide Hill. Horse and rider must then swim across a wide section of the Okanogan River and make their way up a ramp and into the stampede arena.

The race has been a tradition in Omak for more than sixty years, and many race participants are experienced riders from the nearby Colville Indian Reservation, riding horses specially bred for speed and competition. Still, occasionally a horse will fall on the slope and end up having to be put to death. That possibility for disaster alarms animal-rights organizations, but, like car racing, the whiff of danger seems to be what gets spectators to buy event tickets.

The Omak Stampede and Suicide Race is held at the East Side Park each August, on the second weekend of the month. For more information on the events and about the weeklong Indian Encampment that accompanies the festivities, call (800) 933-6625 or log on to www.omak stampede.org.

Root for the Cougars, but Visit the Bears

Pullman

Back in 1927 Washington State University's nationally ranked football team, the Cougars, got its first live cougar cub mascot. Named Butch in honor of one of the team's stars, Herbert "Butch" Meeker, this first cub was followed by Butch II in 1938, twin cubs Butch III and Butch IV in 1942, and Butch V in 1955. Butch VI, who was the team's last live mascot, died in 1978. Today an all-purpose Butch is played by a human in a fuzzy cougar outfit and a large team uniform.

That doesn't mean there aren't any wild animals on campus. In fact, play your cards right and you're likely to find up to a dozen grizzly and black bears in residence at the school's well-fenced-in bear research facility on the edge of campus.

There are eight species of bears worldwide. Sadly, due to man's encroachment on the bears' natural habitats and the practice of hunting bears for sport, six of the species are threatened or endangered. The WSU Bear Research, Education, and Conservation Program, created by Dr. Charles Robbins to gather information about endangered bear populations, is now the only place in the world housing adult grizzly bears for research.

What's it like? The bears have a two-acre exercise yard and six indoor/outdoor pens with temperature-controlled dens. The dens offer cool refuge on hot summer days and a quiet area for winter hibernation. Four adult grizzlies who were orphaned as cubs (Bo, Irving, June, and Patches) live at the facility full-time. Other bears are just visitors who stay for the duration of a specific research project before moving on to zoos or sanctuaries. Occasionally, a black bear that hasn't had too much direct contact with humans is released to the wild.

The bear research facility is located on Airport Road, on the east edge of the Washington State University campus. You can stop by to see if any of the bears are roaming about or call ahead for an official tour of the facility and an educational lecture. (This is, after all, a university.) For more information phone (509) 335-1119 or visit www.natural-resources .wsu.edu/research/bear-center.

THE POWER OF THE POST OFFICE

Although the city of Newport, located on the Washington-Idaho border just west of the Pend Oreille River, is officially in Washington State, it started out in Idaho.

In 1890 a post office opened in a store in Newport, Idaho, near what is now the Pend Oreille River bridge. In 1892 tracks for the Great Northern Railway were laid past the store and a depot was set up in a boxcar. When the depot burned down, however, the replacement building was built three blocks to the west, over the border in Washington State. The town was officially "moved" when the post office announced: "Newport, Idaho, moved 3,175 feet to Newport, Washington."

National Lentil Festival

Pullman

Love lentils? The folks in eastern Washington do. That's because pretty much all the lentils grown commercially in the United States—up to 250 million pounds in a good year—come from eastern Washington and northern Idaho, the area generally known as the Palouse. Bump into a lentil farmer and you'll hear high praise for these little legumes. They're not only low in calories and cholesterol-free, they're full of fiber, potassium, and protein. And fun!

At least that's what the folks who organize the National Lentil Festival in Pullman each August believe. I can't help but agree.

First, there's the lentil mascot. Perky little Tase T. Lentil, who resembles those popular candy-coated chocolates (without the colorful shell), shows up everywhere, including the Lentil Festival Parade. Then there's the Lentil Pancake Breakfast and the Lentil Street Fair, where they dole out free tastes for all from a 200-gallon vat of lentil chili, prepared by the chef from nearby Washington State University.

Other festival highlights include the finals of the National Lentil Festival Cook-off, offering up a surprising array of luscious lentil-laden dishes, with categories for main dishes, salads, soups, snacks, and

The National Lentil Festival lets folks taste lentil-laden treats and meet new lentil-loving friends.

283

desserts. Speaking of dessert, don't miss Lentil Lane, the festival's food court. There you'll find more of that lentil chili, along with lentil pizza, lentil soup, and the very popular lentil ice cream: vanilla ice cream mixed with chocolate-covered lentils. Yum!

The National Lentil Festival is held the fourth weekend in August or on the weekend before students at Washington State University begin classes. For more information call (800) 365-6948 or log on to www.lentilfest.com.

PULLMAN GETS ITS NAME

Pullman was originally platted in 1882 as Three Forks, in honor of its setting at the junction of three streams. Not too long after, the town was renamed in honor of the railroad sleeping-car manufacturer George Pullman, a friend of a local resident. Townspeople agreed to the change, hoping Pullman would contribute money to the town's development. The funds never materialized, but by then the opportunity to change the town's name again had left the station.

Curiosity U
Pullman

Sure, Washington State University's Museum of Art is the largest fine-arts facility in the inland Northwest, but why linger there when there are petrified wood collections, stuffed antelopes, and 8-foot-long soil samples to gawk at elsewhere on campus? The school has more than a dozen museums open to the public and a good number of special collections that researchers are happy to show you by appointment. I've listed just a few of my favorites here. Park the car, grab a map, and explore.

- With more than 2,000 pieces, the Jacklin Petrified Wood Collection in the Physical Sciences Building is the largest display of its kind in the western United States. The Jacklins collected much of the wood themselves on trips around the west, but rumor has it that Lyle Jacklin also had a "connection": a hermit living in the forest who gathered fossilized wood that Jacklin then polished up for his collection. In addition to all the lovely petrified wood on display, this minimuseum features cut and polished agates, geodes, and dinosaur bones as well as the Culver collection of more than one hundred top-grade rock and mineral specimens. Kids especially enjoy stepping behind a curtain to see the wide variety of fluorescent stones light up in neon colors under ultraviolet lights. Phone (509) 335-3009.

- The Charles R. Conner Museum in Abelson Hall first opened in 1894. Back then it featured highlights from two freight-car loads of specimens the state of Washington had exhibited at the 1893 World's Columbia Exposition in Chicago. Now the museum is touted as the best and largest public collection of birds and mammals in the Pacific Northwest. Among the mounted specimens on display are 570 birds, 225 bird eggs, and more than 145 mammals, including a moose, a huge bison, a bighorn sheep, a freeze-dried cow leg, a dinosaur skeleton, and examples of the Pacific Northwest mountain beaver, which turns out to be not a beaver at all but a strange, nonaquatic rodent. Phone (509) 335-3515.

- If you'd rather see the inside of animals, head over to the Robert P. Worthman Veterinary Anatomy Teaching Museum in Room 270 at Wegner Hall. The museum has an outstanding if somewhat grisly collection of anatomical specimens on display, including dissected and freeze-dried sections of horses, cows, sheep, pigs, and one lone llama. If you tend to get queasy or have children in tow, be forewarned that you're also likely to encounter some specimens that have been sliced open to display the innards. For some folks this will be the big attraction. Phone (509) 335-5701.

- The Mycological Herbarium on the third floor of Johnson Hall features more than 70,000 specimens of fungi, including smut fungi, downy mildew, and all sorts of parasitic fungi that can be found throughout the Northwest. Phone (509) 335-9541 or visit http://mycology.wsu.edu/.

- The Maurice James Entomological Collection makes its home, alarmingly, in room 157 of the Food Science and Human Nutrition Building. There are more than 1.25 million specimens of insects and related arthropods and a photographic collection of most any other bug you'd like to see. A display case is filled with some colorful and outsize specimens out front, but it's much more fun if you arrange for a tour of the collection in advance. Phone (509) 335-3394 or log on to http://entomology.wsu.edu/museum/index.html.

- Perhaps the most curious collection on campus is the Smith Soil Monolith Collection, which is housed in what appears to be a converted storage closet in Room 114 in Smith Hall. Switch on the light and look through the observation window to get a look at some of the 150 preserved samples or "profiles" that represent soils from all regions of the state. What you'll see is more than tiny vials of dirt; some of these samples are more than 8 feet long! Phone (509) 335-1859.

All these museums and collections, and a whole bunch more, are scattered around the Washington State University campus. For more information about hours and locations, visit the WSU Visitor Center in downtown Pullman at the corner of State Street and Grand Avenue or stop at the Public Safety Building on campus. You can also call (509) 335-8633 or log on to www.wsu.edu/NIS/LibrariesandMuseums.html.

Dairy to Dream of
Pullman

If you haven't lost your appetite completely at the Worthman Veterinary Anatomy Teaching Museum, you'll probably enjoy a stop at Ferdinand's Dairy Bar, in the Food Quality Building on the campus of Washington State University.

For more than seventy years, the university has kept a hardworking dairy herd on hand to supply the campus creamery with the milk products needed to produce 180,000 cans of cheese each year as well as a variety of other dairy products, including 11,000 gallons of ice cream in twenty flavors.

While the soda fountain is a popular stop for cones and shakes, Ferdinand's is also where folks go to buy Cougar Gold. This tasty cheese, developed on campus in the 1940s, was a by-product of research sponsored by the U.S. government and the American Can Company. Cans were popular back then because plastics weren't yet readily available and wax tended to crack and break. Today, although modern methods can keep cheese from getting moldy, Ferdinand's thirty-ounce canned cheeses remain extremely popular.

Ferdinand's is located in the Food Quality Building on the WSU campus, two blocks east of the Biotech Life Sciences construction site (formerly the Stadium Way Tennis Courts). You can sample the cheese, watch a short video about the cheese-making process, and take a self-guided tour of the creamery. Phone (800) 457-5442 or visit www.wsu .edu/creamery/.

Can You Dig It?
Republic

Sure, you can see fossils in a museum, but that's a stuffy way to learn about prehistoric times. Wouldn't it be much more exciting if you and your family could dig those fossils out of the ground yourselves? Well, you can, if you're willing to head out to the tiny town of Republic in the northeast corner of the state.

Republic was originally known as Eureka, no doubt because gold was discovered in the surrounding hills in 1896. The subsequent rush of gold-seekers swelled the town's population to several thousand people (and more than two dozen saloons), and by 1900 Republic was one of the largest towns in eastern Washington. Since then, most of the mines have closed, and today Republic is a sleepy place with fewer than a thousand residents.

It has oodles of fossils, though. Republic's Stonerose Fossil Site is seemingly chock-full of embedded impressions of plants, insects, and fish that lived in the area more than fifty million years ago. In fact, the earliest known records of the rose and the maple families were found at this site.

See just what sort of fossils other folks have found around here at the Stonerose Interpretive Center, then don your pith helmet and become a fossil hunter yourself by purchasing a day permit to dig around the center's Boot Hill site. You can bring your own tools (a hammer and a chisel) or rent them on-site.

What if you hit pay dirt and dig up a fossil? Each "hunter" is allowed to take home three fossils a day, but you'll need to show your finds to the staff before you leave. Because this is an educational site, if someone digs up something of true scientific value, the artifact is added to the center's permanent collection. Can you dig it?

The Stonerose Interpretive Center and Fossil Site, open from May through October, is located at 15-1 North Kean Street at the corner of State Route 20 West, across from the city park in Republic. For hours, admission, and tool rental fees, call (509) 775-2295 or visit the center online at www.stonerosefossil.org.

Healing Waters and Far-Out Sights
Soap Lake

Just 5 miles northeast of Ephrata there's a lake that Native American tribes called "smokiam," or healing waters. White settlers called it Soap Lake because the seventeen natural minerals in the water give it a soapy feel and, on windy days, a sudsy appearance.

A mix of titanium, aluminum, iron, tungsten, and other minerals gives Soap Lake's water its rare quality. (Supposedly the only other body of water with similar properties is in Germany.) So it's no surprise that in the early 1900s a popular resort area sprang up on shore. Centered around a health retreat called the Soap Lake Sanitorium, a wide variety of hotels and inns catered to folks who flocked here to both drink and bathe in waters that allegedly cured everything from stiff joints and skin diseases to digestive disorders and circulatory problems. After a long day soaking in the lake, many refreshed and revitalized visitors then spent their evenings drinking, dancing, and partying in town.

The Great Depression (and a drought) snuffed out Soap Lake's popularity, but the therapeutic waters and the arid climate still draw a small but steady stream of visitors, many of whom are delighted to discover that Soap Lake water is piped into the bathrooms of several local hotels.

The folks in Soap Lake have their hearts set on building the world's largest lava lamp. We'll have to wait to see what bubbles up.

If the promise of healing bathwater isn't enough to get you to plan a trip to Soap Lake, keep in mind that Brent Blake and some Soap Lake boosters have embarked on a campaign to erect the world's largest lava lamp in town. They envision a 60-foot-tall, 18-foot-diameter lamp filled with giant, slowly undulating blobs of colored goo, complete with a searchlight on top and an observation deck circling the middle.

Sounds groovy, but what's the connection? Promoters say a giant lava lamp would be an interesting and most appropriate way of bringing the lava theme back to an area that was one of the last areas on earth to experience a massive flow of lava.

Unfortunately, building a working 60-foot-tall lava lamp was far too costly. But just when the plug for the project was about to be pulled, the folks at Target Stores called with an intriguing offer. They had a fake 50-foot lava lamp they'd used as an advertisement in New York City and they'd be happy to give it to Soap Lake for free. Sure, it had a big red Target-style bull's-eye inside instead of the hoped-for undulating goo. And sure, it had to be disassembled and shipped across country at quite a cost. But free giant lava lamps don't come along all that often. So a deal was made.

But don't rush over to Soap Lake just yet hoping to see the lava lamp in action. The pieces of the 50-foot structure have been sitting in a warehouse in nearby Ephrata since February 2005 while local officials try to raise enough money to get it put back together.

Soap Lake is situated near the junction of State Routes 17 and 28. For more information about the current status of the giant lava lamp, call (509) 246-1692 or visit www.giantlavalamp.com.

A Little Bit of This and a Lot of That

Spokane

On the yellow foldout photocopy that serves as the advertisement for Marvin Carr's One-of-a-Kind in the World Museum, Carr is referred to as "curator of man's efferent flux in stirring metal." What does that mean? Who knows?! And, really, who cares? Just let twinkly-eyed Carr guide you through his collection of stuff and have fun.

Marvin Carr and one of the celebrity-owned cars he's "captured" for his One-of-a-Kind in the World Museum.

In a nondescript building on the edge of town, Marvin Carr has assembled an eclectic collection of vintage cars, antique furniture, smoking paraphernalia, kooky sculptures, and assorted stuff that has caught his attention as he's made his way through life. Carr loves everything he's "captured" (as he calls it), but his pride and joy is the powder blue 1968 limousine once owned by Jackie Gleason. Ooh and ah a bit and Carr will open the limo's back door so you can sit in the same crushed blue velvet seat where the "Great One" once sat and hear Carr's story about how Gleason outfitted the car to his very specific tastes. Parked elsewhere in the museum is a 1962 Lincoln Continental that once belonged to President John F. Kennedy and a 1973 Lincoln Mark IV that once belonged to Elvis Presley. Carr has stories that accompany the "capture" of these vehicles as well, and he is delighted to share them.

The cars are intriguing, but it's the eclectic nature of Carr's collection that will have you shaking your head. Veering between unusual memorabilia and pure kitsch, the holdings include reverse glass paintings, a Chinese junk made from 27,500 matchsticks, a 13-foot-long replica of a Navy destroyer, and the equally long hide of Fritz, a friend's deceased pet boa constrictor.

Carr's One-of-a-Kind in the World Museum, at 5225 North Freya Street, is open Saturday and Sunday from 1:00 to 4:00 p.m. Admission is charged. For more information phone (509) 489-8859.

Pit Stop for Spitters
Spokane

The Green Bluff Growers represent a community of about twenty-five family farms in the Spokane area where they grow everything from blueberries to Christmas trees. Many of the orchards offer pick-your-own opportunities and family-oriented activities to folks who stop by. The group also sponsors an annual Peach Festival in August and a Cherry Festival each July, which features a Cherry Pickers' Trot, a Tot Trot, and a Cherry Pit Spit.

A Cherry Pit Spit? Yup, there's finally a contest to see who can spit a cherry pit the farthest. And a place where you can debate with others the merits of spitting pits with a rolled or flat tongue. And now you can tell your mom you were just practicing for the big time all those years she scolded you for spitting your cherry pits out onto the lawn.

If you plan on entering the Cherry Pit Spit, be prepared for some stiff competition. Each year more than 500 contestants enter the contest. As of 2006 the women's Pit Spit record holder was Leslie Strake, whose spit pit sailed 32 feet, 9 inches. Mike Stephens, the men's Pit Spit record holder, spit his pit 43 feet, 2 inches. So keep spitting your pits, keep your back to the wind, and you might just end up next year's Pit Spit Champion!

For a map of the orchards and more information about the Green Bluff Growers and the Cherry Pit Spit, call (509) 238-4709 or check the group's Web site, greenbluffgrowers.com.

WHO GOES THERE?

Gonzaga University is named after a sixteenth-century Italian Jesuit, Aloysius Gonzaga. Born in Venice, he died after contracting the plague in Rome not long after he volunteered to try to save other young people from the same fate. Still, Gonzaga was later named the patron saint of youth.

Honorable as his efforts were, if modern-day students follow too closely in the footsteps of Aloysius, they won't get much studying done: it seems that whenever he went up or down stairs, young Aloysius Gonzaga would stop at every step and recite a Hail Mary.

Still, dragging one's heels might be in order at the Monaghan Mansion, the school's music building. Back in 1975, students and staff members started reporting strange occurrences. The supernatural events included a flip-flopping crucifix, a mysterious force field, flute music heard when no flute or flutist was around, and shuffling footsteps on supposedly empty floors.

To put an end to the strange shenanigans, a school staffer resorted to reciting exorcism prayers inside the conservatory. Although it wasn't the formal rite of exorcism, which is performed only by permission of a local bishop, the prayers seemed to do the trick. The unexplained incidents dissipated, but it took more than six sessions of prayers.

Going My Way?

Spokane

Harry Lillis "Bing" Crosby recorded more than 11,000 songs in his long career, acted in more than one hundred films, and hosted numerous network radio and television programs. These days he's best remembered for his crooning voice, for the movies he made with his buddy Bob Hope, and for his roles in such classic films as *The Bells of St. Mary's* and *Going My Way*.

Crosby was born in Tacoma, Washington, and as a kid moved with his family to Spokane, where he later spent a few semesters at Gonzaga University. Although he dropped out before graduating, Crosby nevertheless became a contributing alumnus and was awarded an honorary doctorate in 1937.

Crosby's boyhood home is right next to the Gonzaga campus (the building now houses the Gonzaga Alumni Association). During weekday business hours you can stop by and see a few cases of Crosby-related memorabilia. There's also a statue on the school grounds that depicts a relaxed-looking Crosby complete with a jaunty fedora and golf clubs.

Most intriguing is the jam-packed one-room Bing Crosby museum, officially called the Crosbyana Room, on the first floor of the Crosby Student Center. The museum features a wide variety of items relating to Crosby's life and career, including gold and platinum records, photographs, trophies, plaques, and numerous Crosby-endorsed items, such as a mousetrap and a muscle-building device. Other highlights include a colorful Bing Crosby "Call Me Lucky" board game, an (empty) blue and white box of Bing Crosby ice cream, a bright yellow hockey-puck-size Bing Crosby record cleaner, and a wonderful Bing Crosby coloring book. There's sheet music for tunes Crosby made famous, including

"White Christmas" and "Moonlight Becomes You," along with Crosby's 1945 Oscar for *Going My Way* and a donut-encrusted plaque from the National Dunking Association, which named Crosby "the radio star whose face is most conducive to dunking" during National Donut week in 1949.

True Crosby fans will want to know that with the acquisition of the holdings of the Tacoma-based Bing Crosby Historical Society, Gonzaga University now has the largest public Bing Crosby collection in the world. Although only a small portion of the collection is displayed in the Crosbyana Room, the rest is right next door at the Foley Library. Special-collections librarians are happy to show off some of the photograph albums, clip files, and other items kept in storage.

The Crosbyana Room is in the Crosby Student Center, East 502 Boone Avenue, at Gonzaga University near downtown Spokane. For more information, call (509) 323-4907. Additional information is posted on the museum's Web site, www.gonzaga.edu/Campus-Resources/Museums-and-Libraries/Crosby-Museum.

Don't Fall off This Wagon
Spokane

Kids and adults alike will wonder if they've stumbled into a chapter of *Alice's Adventures in Wonderland* when they come upon the bright red Radio Flyer wagon in Spokane's Riverfront Park. I'm not referring to the chapter in which Alice gets big and everything else shrinks down very small. I'm talking about the part of the story where our heroine gets very, very small and everything else grows very, very large.

The storybook feeling comes from artist Ken Spiering's 12-foot-high, 27-foot-long creation: a red and white version of a child's wagon that is large enough to hold several hundred children and, if they weren't too shy to climb aboard, almost as many adults.

Spiering designed the sculpture as part of a Junior League–sponsored competition seeking artwork for the city's downtown park. Officially titled *The Childhood Express*, this red wagon is a blown-up version of an iconic toy that immediately brings out the kid in everyone. So it's a good thing youngsters are welcome and encouraged to climb up on the wagon and slide right down its handle.

The world's largest red wagon is located in Spokane's Riverfront Park, right near the vintage carousel and another sculpture loved by local children, the garbage-eating goat.

The world's largest red wagon doubles as Spokane's best slide.

What's for Lunch?

Spokane

Sister Paula Mary Turnbull says that her ministry is "the performance and teaching of art."

Born in Seattle and now a member of the Convent of the Holy Names in Spokane, Sister Turnbull has spent most of her life learning about art, teaching art, taking students around the world to see art, and, most notably, making art. These days you're likely to find her, welding torch in hand, in the Holy Names Art Studio.

Turnbull's work ranges from small watercolors to the large metal sculptural pieces that can now be seen in public buildings, churches, gardens, and private homes across the country. In Spokane her well-loved pieces include the *Australian Sundial* on the east end of River-front Park, the *Sasquatch* that sits halfway up the stairwell at the student activity center at Spokane Community College, and, of course, the piece affectionately known by local kids and visitors as "the garbage-eating goat."

Turnbull created the goat sculpture when Spokane hosted the 1974 World's Fair. Known as Expo '74, the fair occupied the one-hundred-acre Riverfront Park, which also now features that giant red wagon and a Looff carousel. Kids love riding the carousel and shooting down the slide of the oversize wagon, of course, but it's a delight to see them running around the park searching for discarded cups and crumpled paper so they can feed trash to the goat, who sucks it up courtesy of a large vacuum apparatus attached to his hindquarters.

The garbage-eating goat sculpture lives in Riverfront Park, in down-town Spokane, not too far from the carousel and the giant red wagon.

Cleaning up is fun.

Super-Sized and Homogenized
Spokane

Boston's Children's Museum may have a 40-foot-tall milk bottle out front, but Spokane has it beat with two novelty buildings shaped like giant milk bottles.

In the 1930s Paul Newport, owner of the Benewah Creamery, had big plans: He announced to the local newspaper that he was going to spend $25,000 to build six new shops around town, and that each one would be shaped like a giant milk bottle. Newport hired a noted architectural firm to design the shops, which were to be 38 feet tall and 15 feet across and would look just like the "little" bottles folks poured milk from at home.

Newport succeeded in building only two of the giant milk bottles before his creamery business went sour, but maybe that was enough. Each was made from metal and cement, covered with stucco, painted white, and trimmed with neon tubing.

Both attention-grabbing buildings are still standing. One is a retail shop; the other is, more appropriately, a popular ice-cream and burger joint called Mary Lou's Milk Bottle Restaurant. The restaurant-in-the-round serves burgers, fries, and lots and lots of Mary Lou's Ice Cream in cones, cups, sundaes, milk shakes, floats, and malts. Just the sort of thing you'd want from a giant milk bottle, right?

Mary Lou's Milk Bottle Restaurant is located in Spokane's Garland District, at 802 West Garland Avenue at Post Street. The other milk-bottle building is near downtown Spokane, at Cedar Street, between Third and Fourth Streets. For hours and more information call (509) 325-1772.

Got milk? Six milk-bottle-shaped buildings were originally planned for Spokane, but only two got built.

NEED A TIE?

Although a visitor from outer space might think it's a special day on which men are presented with gaudily wrapped ties, the third Sunday in June, thanks to a woman from Spokane, is actually the day Americans honor their dads.

Sonora Smart Dodd was a young girl in Spokane when her mom died, leaving her dad, Civil War veteran William Jackson Smart, to raise the family's six kids alone. He must have done a pretty good job, because in 1909, when she was twenty-seven years old, Sonora started a campaign to have the entire nation set aside one day each year just to honor fathers.

At first she was ridiculed, but the woman known in Spokane for being a poet, a writer, and a sculptor persevered. On June 19, 1910, with the support of local civic and religious organizations, Spokane observed the first Father's Day.

News of this special day soon spread around the country. In 1914 Congress passed a Father's Day resolution, and in 1972 President Richard Nixon made Father's Day a national holiday.

While speaking to those who gathered for the 1965 dedication of a plaque being installed to commemorate her efforts, Dodd said that on that first Father's Day "groups of Spokane women prepared home dinners . . . and made gifts for shut-in fathers." Today, as we all know, the more appropriate way to thank our dads for everything they've done for us is to buy a tie, make a quick phone call, or send a card. In fact, according to the Greeting Card Association, close to one hundred million Father's Day cards are purchased and mailed each year. There's no official estimate, however, on how many ties Sonora Smart Dodd's father ended up with.

Pigeonhole Parking and Square-Wheeled Tractors
Spokane

In 1924 mechanical wizard and restless inventor Royal Newton Riblet
built himself a mansion on a terrace of volcanic rock overlooking the
Spokane River. Riblet called his sumptuous three-story red-tiled home
"Eagle's Nest" and had it wired for all the latest electronic gadgetry,
including a then unheard-of electric log for the fireplace. On the
grounds he installed a waterfall, a sloped 60,000-gallon basalt swimming pool, a private airstrip, a ski
slope, a croquet court, an
archery range, a put-
ting green, and a
life-size
checker-
board.

No problem finding a parking space if you've got pigeonhole parking in town.

Out front, there was a steel gate, and attached to the gate was a mailboxlike contraption that brought the mail to the main house via a miniature electric train. Out back, there was a five-passenger tram that ran back and forth from the valley, over the Spokane River, and up to the house. Fishing poles were kept onboard so visitors could try to catch something in the river on their trip across. A Spokane landmark until it was dismantled in 1956, Riblet's tram ran on a standard car engine, transmission, clutch, and starter. That meant no special operator was needed to run the tram because anyone familiar with controls in a car could make it move.

Riblet's creativity wasn't limited to his home. He held more than twenty patents for all manner of inventions. His most notable creation was the square wheel, which laid down several flat segments of track as it turned. Attached to a tractor, this sort of wheel offered better traction and caused less erosion than traditional field machinery. In fact, in 1942 the United States Army conducted tests using Riblet's invention and declared it a suitable accessory for wartime transportation.

Riblet also put his mind to solving the problem of where to park cars in crowded urban centers. He invented "pigeonhole parking," which eliminated the familiar space-hogging ramps in high-rise parking garages and made room for twice as many cars. His solution? Pigeonhole parking garages used a mechanical lift to deliver and remove cars from stacked parking slots.

The inventor didn't limit himself to tractors and automobiles. When his daughter, Virginia, was just eighteen months old, her dad made her a miniature bicycle that was the smallest pneumatic-tired cycle in the world.

Royal Riblet died in 1960, and today his Eagle's Nest mansion is the home of the Arbor Crest Wine Cellars, which welcomes visitors to tour the grounds, marvel at the square-wheeled tractor, walk around the checkerboard, look out over the river, and sip a glass of wine while contemplating Royal Riblet's ingenuity.

Arbor Crest Wine Cellars is located at 4705 Fruithill Road in Spokane. For directions and information about hours and events, call (509) 927-9463 or visit www.arborcrest.com.

Ghostly Guests
Spokane

When it opened in September 1914, Spokane's grand Davenport Hotel was a marvel. Built at a cost of $3 million, the 405-room Davenport boasted that it was the first hotel with air-conditioning, a central vacuum system, housekeeping carts, and accordion ballroom doors. Elevators were state-of-the-art and public spaces were lavish, with grand ballrooms, elegant restaurants and lounges, and a huge, elegant lobby surrounded by a mezzanine and covered by a skylight.

The place to be seen—then and now.

During its heyday the hotel welcomed royalty from around the world, captains of commerce and industry, and celebrities of every stripe, including just about every American president of the twentieth century, Charles Lindbergh, Mary Pickford, Clark Gable, Bob Hope, Bing Crosby, and Benny Goodman. And although the hotel fell into disrepair and closed in 1985, it narrowly escaped demolition and reopened, fully restored, in 2002.

Since then many former guests have stopped by to see the stunning ballrooms and the lovingly refurbished lobby. At least one of the hotel's ghosts seems to have found its way back as well. As they did for decades before the hotel closed, modern-day guests see a woman dressed in 1920s fashion, wandering along the mezzanine and peering over the railing as if she's looking for someone in the lobby below. The mysterious woman is thought to be the ghost of Mrs. Ellen McNamara, who fell to her death through the lobby skylights during the dinner hour on Tuesday evening, August 17, 1920.

Mrs. McNamara and the other ghosts said to walk the halls of the hotel aren't mentioned in the official Historical Walking Tour brochure posted on the hotel's Web site (www.davenporthotel.com) and available for free at the front desk, but many hotel staff members are familiar with the stories and are happy to share them. The Davenport Hotel is at 10 South Post Street in downtown Spokane. For more information call (800) 899-1482.

Washington's Oldest Diner

Spokane

In a city studded with rare roadside architecture that includes two giant milk-bottle buildings and a trio of shops and homes in the shape of windmills, a classic diner can go unnoticed.

These days Frank's Diner is well known for serving mighty breakfasts featuring omelettes that contain up to a half dozen eggs. The diner's biggest claim to fame, however, is that it's the oldest diner in the state. The wood-paneled eatery was first put into service as a railroad dining car back in 1906. It then served as an off-track hash house in Seattle from the 1930s through the early 1990s before being moved to Spokane, where you can eat at the counter or snuggle into a booth in the back.

Frank's Diner now sits at 1516 West Second Avenue. Phone (509) 747-8798 or visit www.franksdiners.com.

Fueling the Imagination
Spokane

In the early 1900s the Forest Service began building fire lookout stations throughout the Pacific Northwest, eventually placing 466 staffed lookouts throughout Washington State. At first, many of these structures were nothing more than wooden platforms in trees, with crude access ladders nailed to the trunks. Later on, the lookout towers were more elaborate cabinlike structures with wraparound windows, but rarely were they equipped with running water or much else in the way of creature comforts.

No smoking please!

EASTERN WASHINGTON

For about fifty years fire lookout jobs were a perfect match for folks who liked reading, writing, and being totally alone on a mountaintop for long stretches of time. In fact, in 1956 Beat generation writer Jack Kerouac spent sixty-three days watching for fires from the lookout at Desolation Peak in the North Cascades National Park. He later wrote about the experience in *Dharma Bums* and *Desolation Angels*. Another Beat–era writer, Gary Snyder, who also enjoyed the lookout towers, used his time on Sourdough Mountain above Diablo Lake to write many of his early poems. Today these lookouts have been added to the National Historic Lookout Register (see www.firetower.org).

These days fires are mostly monitored from the air, and just a few lookout towers in Washington State remain staffed during the summer. While most lookouts have fallen into disrepair, some hiking groups have started adopting and restoring towers, turning at least one into a museum and others into rugged overnight accommodations. For information about several lookouts available for overnight rentals in Washington, visit www.fs.fed.us/r6/recreation/rentals.

If you're in eastern Washington, stop by the Fire Lookout Museum outside of Spokane. Operated by Ray and Rita Kresek, the museum owns three lookout towers (two are on-site); more than 1,400 Smokey Bear–related items; and more than 3,000 objects related to fire detection and wildfire protection, including a 1953 fire truck, vintage fire tools, all manner of weather instruments and communication devices, and lots more. The museum is located 7 miles north of Spokane at 123 W Westview, ¼ mile northwest of the "Y" junction of US 2 and US 395. For more information call (509) 466-9171 or visit www.firelookouts.com.

Rolling Along but Getting Nowhere
Uniontown

It's not as if Steve and Junette Dahmen don't have enough to do at their farm alongside U.S. Highway 195 in Uniontown, south of Pullman. It's just that once they got going, their collection of iron wheels kept on rolling along.

The wheels on this wagon-wheel fence don't do anything or go anywhere, but that's just fine with the Dahmens of Uniontown.

The Dahmens have wheels from almost anything that ever had them, including baby buggies, threshing machines, tractors, manure spreaders, and old mail wagons. Over the years they've bought some wheels themselves, but other folks have brought over their interesting-looking and antique specimens as well. One man from Idaho gave the Dahmens a 6 foot wheel that he discovered while digging a basement for his new home. Another fellow donated huge wheels from the steam engines his father had collected.

The wheels don't just get piled up around the Dahmens' property They're put to good and imaginative use as elements in an ever-lengthening fence that snakes its way up the hill in the pasture, encircles a vegetable garden and a little park, and winds back around the house.

All told, there are more than 1,000 wheels in what is more fanciful sculpture than utilitarian railing. Some smaller wheels that are placed on top of larger ones seem to be rolling along the top of the fence. Unusual wheels, such as the ones with curved wooden spokes, stand out in a stretch of roundness. And, say the Dahmens, the scene framed by the fence changes with each season. Snow-lined wheels create lacy designs in the winter, and each spring only the topmost fence wheels are visible from the road.

The Dahmens enjoy it when passersby pull their cars over to marvel at the unusual creation, take pictures, and write a note in the guest book, which is filled with enthusiastic comments from visitors from all over the world.

To see the wagon-wheel fence, head south from Pullman about 15 miles on US 195.

Sweet as an Onion?
Walla Walla

Walla Walla, a Native American word meaning "many waters," is not just a nice place to visit. This southeast Washington city is home to a curious variety of onion that makes people smile instead of cry.

More than a century ago, French soldier Peter Pieri picked up some sweet onion seeds on the island of Corsica, off the west coast of Italy. He brought some of those seeds with him to the Walla Walla Valley where, over several generations, area farmers have developed what is now the area's specialty crop of onions that are consistently large, round, and unusually juicy and sweet. Today about sixty farmers grow Walla Walla Sweet Onions on 800 to 1,000 acres of land.

"Oh no, now one of us has to go home and change."

Walla Walla Sweet Onions aren't sweet because they're full of sugar, but because they're 90 percent water and contain about half as much sulfur as the more familiar yellow onions we throw in our soups. So although it may look strange, it's not unusual to see folks bite into a Walla Walla sweet onion in the same way others might enjoy an apple.

Fun with onions doesn't end there. Each July downtown Walla Walla hosts the Walla Walla Sweet Onion Festival at Pioneer Park. At one time the festival sponsored a Bald as an Onion competition, but now awards are presented for the largest and most pristine onions, for great onion art, and for recipes that use onions in the most creative ways.

To find out more about Walla Walla Sweet Onions and the festival, call (877) WWVISIT or check out www.wallawalla.org or www.sweet onions.org.

WALLA WALLA CLAIMS TO FAME

- Twenty-five trees scattered around town are the biggest of their kind in the state. Most notable among these is a catalpa tree on the Whitman College campus with a circumference of 21 feet.

- In operation since 1907 the Walla Walla Symphony Orchestra is the oldest continuous symphony west of the Mississippi.

- Dry those tears: In 2007, after a strong lobbying by area students, the Walla Walla Sweet Onion was officially declared Washington's state vegetable.

Do You Know the Muffler Man?
Walla Walla

About thirty years ago, when Mike Hammond opened Melody Muffler, a shop specializing in straightforward mufflers, welding, and vehicle hitch attachments, he needed something to draw attention to his business. So he welded together a few assorted pieces of old mufflers and scrap metal and made a muffler man to put up in front of his shop. He thought maybe he'd get folks to slow down and notice his shop, but instead he set out on a new career in "industrial road art."

"The muffler man looked kind of lonely," says Hammond, "so I built him a wife, Muffy." After a while the muffler couple looked lonely too, so Hammond went to work to create Son of Muffler Man and a cute little dog named Spotweld.

Some folks in town were alarmed by Muffy's oil-funnel breasts, but most fell in love with the entire Muffler family. Soon Hammond had orders from people who wanted their own muffler creations. Happy to oblige, Hammond now spends much of his time visiting scrap metal yards looking for materials to use in his projects, which range from abstract creations to garden bugs, space bugs, yard birds, elephants, dinosaurs, and all manner of metal creatures. Hammond made a metal fisherman for the Walla Walla Worm Ranch and a kooky coffee butler for the Coffee Connection on Main Street. His Lone Ranger, dubbed the Loan Arranger, stood in a bank lobby before a local judge took it home.

Hammond, who also plays in a band called the Iguana Hat Band and runs his own recording studio, usually has the waiting room at Melody Muffler filled with his creations. He takes full responsibility for that wild art car parked out in front, which sports a guy with a torch and assorted wacky things welded to the roof. He's also becoming something of a well-known folk artist: *Tonight Show* host Jay Leno owns one of Hammond's pieces, and his work has been featured in *National Geographic* and in a book describing the nationwide muffler man "movement."

Mike Hammond's muffler men may be metal-heads, but they're well-read.

To see Mike Hammond's muffler art, head to 429 South Ninth Street at the corner of Chestnut Street in Walla Walla. Phone (509) 525-7036 or log on to www.mikehammond.com.

INDEX

INDEX

INDEX

INDEX

INDEX

INDEX

INDEX

About the Author

Harriet Baskas is a writer and an award-winning radio producer. She's been the manager of several community radio stations and now produces stories about unusual museums and hidden museum collections for public radio. She has written several books, including *Oregon Curiosities* (Globe Pequot), *Museums of the Northwest* (Sasquatch Books), and *Stuck at the Airport* (Simon & Schuster). If someone else had gotten the assignment to write this book, Harriet would have campaigned to have her collection of hankies-of-the-states featured in it.